AN ELUSIVE PERSPECTIVE

AN INTRODUCTION TO WAKING THE FUCK UP

FRANKLIN OROZCO

Copyright © 2025 by Lucid Perspective LLC

All rights reserved.

No portion of this book may be reproduced in any form without written permission from the publisher or author, except as permitted by U.S. copyright law.

This publication is designed to provide accurate and authoritative information in regard to the subject matter covered. It is sold with the understanding that neither the author nor the publisher is engaged in rendering legal, investment, accounting or other professional services. While the publisher and author have used their best efforts in preparing this book, they make no representations or warranties with respect to the accuracy or completeness of the contents of this book and specifically disclaim any implied warranties of merchantability or fitness for a particular purpose. No warranty may be created or extended by sales representatives or written sales materials. The advice and strategies contained herein may not be suitable for your situation. You should consult with a professional when appropriate. Neither the publisher nor the author shall be liable for any loss of profit or any other commercial damages, including but not limited to special, incidental, consequential, personal, or other damages.

ISBN: 979-8-9921512-0-6 (paperback)
ISBN: 979-8-9921512-2-0 (hardcover)
ISBN: 979-8-9921512-1-3 (ebook)

Library of Congress Control Number: 2024925812

Book Cover Art & Illustrations are a collaboration by Franklin Orozco & ChatGPT

1st edition January 2025

www.elusiveperspective.com

*In a world full of people, only some want to fly
isn't that crazy?*

-Seal

CONTENTS

FOUNDATIONS 10

Can I Pet That Wabbit? 12
- We've Just Entered Hypnagogia 17
- Objective & Subjective Reality 22
- Frequency and Vibration 32
- The Biology of Belief 39

ILLUSIVE ILLUSIONS 48

You've Been Asleep, Neo 50

The Illusion of Scarcity 56
- Natural Law Proves Abundance 60
- Money Follows the Rules Too 66
- We All Don't Want the Same Things 74

The Illusion of Depression 80

The Illusion of Information 90
- Our Food Is Poison 93
- American Politics 101
- Propagandist Narratives 109
- The Land of Confusion 120

The Illusion of Race 128
- The Identity Wars 131

- The Vilification of the Races 137
- We Are Not Our Physical Bodies 149

LUCID PERSPECTIVES 156

- Manifesting 158
  - Which Type of Manifestor Are You? 160
  - Manifestation 101 167
- Gratitude 172
  - Be Grateful Now, So You Can Be Grateful Later 179
  - Solutions Will Reign Down Upon You 181
- Fear of Failure 188
- Logic vs Emotion 200
  - Pros & Cons of Logic 206
  - Pros & Cons of Emotion 208
  - Logic And Emotion Harmonized 210

LUCID CONCLUSIONS 214

- The Outcome Architect 216

Books You Should Read 227

About the Author 231

An Elusive Perspective

FOUNDATIONS

An Elusive Perspective

Can I Pet That Wabbit?

You're tired and you're fed up. I get it. Our news is full of nonsensical bullshit. Jobs aren't paying anything worth a damn. Bills stack up nonstop and unexpected expenses find ways into your mailbox on top of it. Everyone is addicted to social media for mindless and numbing entertainment. Nobody is listening, nobody cares, nobody seems to be in control of anything and the world is a lonely cruel place so what's the point of all this anyway? Despite all of this, you are holding this book in your hands and there's a small scrap of hope inside you that knows it should and can be better out here. Or perhaps you currently don't have any gripes with your life, and this is light bedtime reading. Either way, please allow me to congratulate you on being born on Earth. All jokes aside, if this first paragraph described your world view, I'm honestly glad you're here. This book is exactly for you! If you hold the totally opposing view of this first paragraph, you may have already completed some major work in your life and that too warrants congratulations.

This cynical and gloomy perspective of the world is extremely common. But what if I told you, it's actually the furthest from the truth? What if I told you there is another way to view the world? I feel like Morpheus when he met Thomas Anderson for the first time in the original Matrix. You're Thomas Anderson; a person who knows something is off but could never quite put a finger on it. You've followed all the subtle hints and clues that have brought you here, to this moment. I'm about to give you the choice of picking the blue pill, or the red pill. The analogy of that scene is relative because I believe we each have a moment like this in our lives, whether we recognize it or not. Of course, if you've never seen the Matrix then this analogy means nothing and I am clearly judging you on your pure lack of knowledge and taste in timeless cinema, but I digress. Allow me to explain. In this scene, Morpheus, the wise and powerful freedom fighter and mentor, is enlightening Thomas, the naïve yet skeptical protagonist, about making a choice to know the truth about reality or to continue to be ignorant and stay in oblivious bliss. He's suspicious because he knows something is off, but he's never had anyone or anything tangible to show him. Picking the blue pill is to choose to learn nothing and change nothing. Picking the red pill is to learn the truth, change your life forever and never going back to the lack of knowledge.

This is your moment. You can put this book down now, and walk away, and not change a thing about your life, environment, or perspective; OR you can keep reading and pop the red pill because deep down you know there isn't any going back from here. You want more fulfillment, you want to understand how to do this, and you want to learn how to make sense of the nonsense in this world.

An Elusive Perspective

In my heart, I believe that the information and the secrets of the universe are out there for those who seek it. But *ONLY* for those who seek it. You may stumble along the way. You may have already test-driven different religions, or spiritual beliefs on your journey. What no one can take from you is that you are an active seeker. Believe it or not, there is virtue in this. You will evolve along the way; this is inevitable. Don't misunderstand me. I am not claiming to know all the secrets of the universe. How could I? I am a living and breathing human being in this realm just as you are. And honestly, I don't think there's anyone on Earth that fully knows all the secrets of the universe, but I do believe there are some people that are much closer than most. There also seems to be a built-in cap on what we could know while we are here due to the nature of why we are here, and I believe we all can somewhat sense it. Can't you? Can't you sense that abundance of knowledge on the edge of your mind that you know has the answers, but you just can't access? I do. I'm not sure if any of us will ever be able to fully access that data bank, but while we're here there are definitely some cheat codes spread throughout the map of this world for us to find. There is a lot of useful information about reality and this life that is purposefully held from us. I don't make the claim that this book has it all, but I'm beyond confident this is a great place to start. After all, this is An Elusive Perspective: An Introduction to Waking the Fuck Up.

We've Just Entered Hypnagogia

Relax, I promise this won't be difficult reading, but I will use big and different words from time to time. Hypnagogia is that state of mind when you're between fully awake and fully asleep. When you may "hallucinate" people, beings and what seems to be another place that's like here, but "different". You've been asleep, Neo. Actually, we're all asleep. There are just many different levels of "sleep". I imagine you'll know which level of sleep you were, hopefully by the end of this book. Or maybe not, it may still take you some time even after putting this book down.

For me, looking back at my past self beyond 15 or so years ago, I was *"sleep-sleep"*. Being asleep in this context is being completely unaware of the possibilities of beneficial perspectives and information available to you. Put more bluntly, my definition of being asleep is being an ill-informed person that believes they know everything there is to know based off their own experiences, environment or mainstream media consumption. For example, the first 15 years of my life, all I really knew was living in the projects of the Bronx. The Bronx was planet Earth and all of existence for me. Of course, I learned in school about the other 49 states and other countries and continents, but in my Mind, they may as well have just been distant areas of The Bronx. I wasn't well traveled at that time, and I had no other experience of other cities, states or countries, so I was very limited in my perception of what the rest of the world could possibly be like. You could say I was "asleep" regarding the entire rest of the world. Today, I have traveled and experienced many places and now know there are countless interesting countries and cities to visit and live in. Some I have lived and experienced firsthand. This awareness could have only come with time and experience but most importantly *EXPOSURE*.

The best way for the information in this book to resonate with you is to understand that you have been asleep at the wheel to most of the possibilities of perception and information available to you. When I was living in New York, all those other cities and countries I've visited later in life were always there. Just because I had never been anywhere else didn't mean those places didn't exist. Think of the information in this book the same way. Every perception, every viewpoint exists out there in the world. There's so much information that exists; It's always been out there, whether you were aware of it or not. Unfortunately, the opposite is also very true. There are distorted perceptions and false information deliberately distributed for purposes of keeping you in a sleep state as the recipient. They can oppress you by placing a veil over your eyes and directing you towards that which does not serve you. They can also oppress you by outright harming you physically, mentally, and spiritually. There are belief systems, propaganda & narratives that are very common, that are spread only for the purpose of deception. Oh, and deceive you they do. In one way or another they have deceived us all.

One request, before you move on, open your mind. The one thing that the Matrix counts on is for closed minds to remain closed when new and beneficial information is trying to get through. Oh, what's the Matrix you say? Good question. You will find that I shall be referencing the Matrix a lot. In the context of this book the Matrix is not the movie anymore; the matrix is the systems. The systems of control, of industry, of authority, of mass media, of politics, of academia, of economics, and many others. When you turn on your television for the news, you have entered the matrix. When you open that glamour magazine, you are reading the matrix. When you open up that social media app on your cell phone, you have activated the matrix. Morpheus said it best:

"It is the world that has been pulled over your eyes to blind you from the truth."

If you read that in Morpheus' voice, we are now friends. Understand, this information has been looking for you. It wants you to be aware of it. It wants to help you become an enlightened being here on Earth. But it can't enter a closed mind. A closed mind is a vault that will not be swayed with any new paradigms outside of what it already believes to be true. This is how most people operate. They received one set of instructions from the matrix, installed the programming and have not received any updates, upgrades or patches. Before you read on, we need to configure some changes in order to undo this programming, otherwise you may as well put this book down now and throw back the blue pill.

Objective & Subjective Reality

We can't possibly begin this journey without first laying out some foundations and discussing the principles of the natural universe that are unchanging and irrefutable. For the purposes of this section, we will call this "Objective Reality." For those who may be unaware, objective reality is what *IS*, regardless of anyone's opinion, bias, or interpretation. There is no argument to be had and no quarrels to be made. One example of objective reality is if you plant a healthy apple seed into fertile soil and water it, in a field which allows plenty of sunlight, that seed will grow into an apple tree that will produce thousands of apples over its lifetime, which can in turn produce hundreds of thousands of apple seeds with the potential to do the same. Irrefutable. Of course, there are many things that can go wrong during the life span of the apple tree. It can be cut down. It can become diseased and die. It can get stomped on when it just begins to sprout. All of that does not matter, the objective reality remains. Another much simpler objective reality (and one I probably should've started with) is the sun rises in the east and sets in the west. This is the same for everyone, everywhere. This cannot be debated or argued. It is a truth no matter who challenges it. You might want to argue who's to say which way is east or west, and that would be an argument of semantics. The coast that the sun rises on and sets is the same for everyone on this planet. It happens whether we as humans wish to acknowledge it or not.

I strongly consider our collective objective reality to be a direct result of a higher intelligence. Call it what you will. Some would say God, Allah, the Universe, The Force, or even perhaps our higher selves. These are all valid monikers and fit the description quite well. For the purposes of this book, I will personally call this intelligence *The Universe*. Please feel free to use whatever reference you please for yourself as you read. The reason I consider objective reality to be a direct result of a higher intelligence, or the Universe is because it does not require anything from us to perform; we are only ever observers of its magnificence. That apple seed does not need our presence for it to do what it does. In fact, nature in general does quite well with or without our influence at all (trust me). There are many aspects of this objective reality that we have observed that require nothing from us in order for it to just be, and I believe these things are governed by an intelligence way above our pay grades here on Earth. The responsibility of those things just does not fall upon us. The Sun rising and setting; does not need us. The wind blowing, rivers flowing, leaves falling; these are aspects of this reality which we do not control. So, this I attribute to that higher intelligence. It is there, and it is very present, whether you want to believe it or not. Remember, objective reality doesn't require your endorsement. You may want to argue what to call this higher intelligence and that is obviously open for interpretation, but the fact remains there is something surrounding us and within us that is governing all the things that we ourselves are not in control of.

Some of you may subscribe to atheist principles or the chaos theory of existence which states there is no God, or higher intelligence or "intelligent designer" and that all we see has occurred as a massive accident of coincidence, luck, fluke and fuckery. I personally find this very hard to ingest due to the complexities of nature and life alone. The apple seed example for instance, is repeatable. I can't agree with associating recurring natural processes with chaos. To me, I personally have no choice but to interpret that as intention. I am not endorsing any organized religion or deity. I believe in a higher intelligence which maintains facets of our reality that we do not have authority over in our present awareness. Chaos cannot describe objective reality. The sun doesn't rise from any direction it chooses on any given day. The sun has a pattern in our sky, it's repeatable, and it's been doing it for eons. The atheist and chaos folks would have you believe that your life, this planet, our solar system and Universe is all here by one gigantic chaotic accident. Arguments can be made for chaotic events, such as tsunamis, tornadoes or hurricanes for instance, but even those have cause, effect and a repeatable pattern. They may seem chaotic to us for obvious reasons, but they are still functioning and purposeful processes of the Earth. One last caveat for the atheists; I'm not saying you must believe in a God or deity. What I am saying is that objective reality shows us that "something" has authority of the things about our reality that we do not. You can call it the Universe, the force, source, the source field, etc. There is a plethora of names for it if you don't want to use God, Allah and all the rest. The bottom line is it is there, and it is unapologetic in its authority and presence.

Since objective reality doesn't require our validation, interpretation or permission, then what exactly are we as humans on Earth, in control of? I'm glad you asked. This has been the topic of much debate over the decades and centuries and for good reason. This is where subjective reality comes in. Subjective reality is that which can be perceived in many different ways by many different people. In other words, subjective reality is how one can view the world through their own eyes, irrespective of how others see the world. I propose that subjective reality is in fact a fractal form of objective reality. There are currently 8 billion human souls on this planet, each with their own experiences. That's 8 billion subjective realities; 8 billion separate "worlds"

An Elusive Perspective

existing here, all at once sharing a single overseeing objective reality that sits upon our personal experiences. Think about your views and beliefs about the world. Think about your political views. Think about your core values. Now understand that there is at least one person on this planet who opposes your every viewpoint, core value and political belief and you both are living here on this same planet breathing this same air. This person could be standing right next to you right now and you both exist in two completely different "realities" yet within the same one objective reality.

    How is this possible? We're going to get into all that, but I first wanted to illustrate that this is the struggle that we all collectively live within our day to day lives. It is also in this conundrum that we find the answer to all our problems. It is each our own subjective reality with which we find we have the most control of our own lives. Before I forget, I never answered the question proposed earlier. What exactly are we in control of? We, my young padawan, are in control of *ourselves*. That is literally it. Objective reality is to absolutely *Zero* control, whereas subjective reality is to *Absolute* control. In case the point hasn't been driven in clearly, I need you to understand. You are only and solely in control of yourself and ironically this is all you need to be in control of to live your best life. This level of control includes your actions, your behaviors, your responses and much more. The most important thing that you have control of, and which defines virtually everything that has happened or will ever happen to you is your *THOUGHTS*. Total control of one's own mind is to have absolute control of your very own personal reality. Each and every one of us does this already whether we know it or not.

All of us, living here in this plane of existence are taking part in two realities (It's really a few more but we're keeping it simple for now, this is the intro book after all). A reality we cannot control, "objective reality" and a reality we cannot help but control, "subjective reality." You, Me, all of us, are

An Elusive Perspective

in total and complete control of our subjective truths and reality. The biggest obstacle to overcome when awakening to this, is learning where your "ideas" truly originated from. How much is actually you, and how much was downloaded and installed by the matrix. Regardless of the ratio, you are still running those programs. As you read throughout this book, we will go over some of the natural laws of the universe and explain how they are applicable. Keep in mind, these laws are irrefutable, and they are the crux and foundation of the concepts being talked about. What better resource to use than nature and natural law to help us understand how to best life? What could be more beneficial to forge these lessons into your mind than to use the tales and anecdotes that nature has bestowed upon us? Doth mother know you weareth her drapes? (Sorry, I couldn't help that). The point I'm making is there is a strong foundation in nature that we must consider, because our subjective realities mimic objective reality and also because it's the only template we have to use.

So, what is the relationship between the two realities? Our subjective reality and thoughts are sent out into the objective reality for processing and eventually execution. Think about it. Objective reality does not need us to perform, but it is a level or dimension above us. This means we can feed it information. Scientifically, lower dimensions provide information to higher dimensions and higher dimensions dictate parameters of lower dimensions. Using nature as an example, think of how the cells in our very own bodies are capable of sending our brain information and our brain dictates movement to the body. Here's a piece of information you probably never heard of or considered before. When we feed this higher intelligence our thoughts, it has no choice but to execute on this information and feed it back to us in the form of the subjective reality that we created! This is the *HACK!* I first learned this over 15 years ago. And over these past 15 years my own life has changed drastically and to my own will. This might be hard to understand now, but I promise give it some time and keep reading.

Frequency and Vibration

Scientists have long discovered that everything in our universe is in motion through vibrations and manifests to our senses as frequencies. The molecules of everything are constantly doing the happy dance of existence. Physical objects, your body, your thoughts, photons of light, molecules and atoms; literally everything. If it can be perceived by our senses, then it is here because it is vibrating at the frequency that we can perceive. Otherwise, it would not be perceivable to us here. This concept translates to us on individual levels as well. Positive experiences, money, relationships, these things cannot exist in our lives if we are not vibrating at the resonating frequencies of these things. If it is not present in your life, you are not resonating at the frequency required to attract it. Think of the 8 billion subjective realities we talked about; each person is essentially their own universe. For most of us, our desires figuratively speaking do exist in an alternate "universe" and we are aware of them, but they haven't manifested for us yet. We can prove this because we know there are people living their lives in abundance and freedom. When you turn on the television and see a person with wealth, we are peering into the experience of a totally different universe than our own, and we see that there are individuals living abundantly. This is not to say it's just celebrities of course. There are plenty of nameless millionaires and billionaires who are living out their dreams. There are also plenty of people without money living fruitful and happy lives. Those experiences exist in this world and because we know that, we know it is also a possibility for us.

I can imagine you feel at times helpless and that no positive outcomes are coming your way, and it is this constant present vibration which brings you little to no positive outcomes. The energy you broadcast off and out into the Universe is what the Universe broadcasts back to you in the form of experiences and circumstance; without question and without fail. What you need to do is understand how you are vibrating and what frequency you are putting out.

Let's thought experiment this down to practical terms. Both a Bugatti and a Fiat have a frequency in this realm. These two vehicles are both quite capable of taking you from point A to point B. The difference is the frequency and vibration of these physical objects. Everyone would agree that Bugatti's are an expensive luxury vehicle that the extremely wealthy generally get to enjoy, while Fiats are quite the opposite. But it's not the price tag alone that makes them different. I would argue it is our collective perception of these vehicles which makes one seem less attainable and more attractive than the other. The fact is both vehicles are equally attainable by just about anyone. Why? Simply put, because they are both here. They are perceivable by everyone alive on this planet. We can say this because we know there are people currently driving Bugatti's and also driving Fiats at this very moment. This is the objective truth. Say it again with me, in this very moment, there are at least two people on Earth; one driving a Bugatti, and one driving a Fiat. The comparison comes from our perceived monetary value of the vehicles which then translates into our perception of which one is harder to obtain. Most people would naturally go for the Fiat than the Bugatti because of their perception of what they can afford and the frequency of what their mind is able to attract. The plot twist is you can obtain any car that exists in this realm, because it is here, and so are you. If you are vibrating at the resonating frequency of a Bugatti, you will be physically driving a Bugatti. If you are vibrating at the resonating frequency of a Fiat, you will be physically driving a Fiat. Right now, think of the vehicle you drive, and then say it with me:

"I vibrate at the resonating frequency of a (your car model), because I drive a (your car model)."

We know this because you are driving that car. Once you understand this concept of "your present vibration equals your present reality" you will be in more control and awareness of your thoughts and emotions! Unfortunately, this is hard for many people to accept because most people can't fathom that the reason their lives aren't panning out is due to the frequency they are vibrating in real time, or that they have any responsibility for their lives at all. The onus is on the individual to accept responsibility for their own frequency and switch the channel. Without accepting responsibility for the channel you are on, you will not change. This is because your reality comes from within you and propagates to the outside (perceived) environment. Here's another exercise you can use to gauge your current vibration. Using the example above with the car, make statements about your current situation and correlate it to your frequency. Here are some examples:

"I vibrate at the resonating frequency of a (condo, house, apartment, trailer, etc.), because I live in a (condo, house, apartment, trailer, etc.)".

"I vibrate at the resonating frequency of a (good, bad, ok, happy, non-existent, etc.) relationship, because I am in a (good, bad, ok, happy, non-existent, etc.) relationship".

Try these with different aspects of your life. Say the statements out loud so they have power. You

An Elusive Perspective

need to understand how massive your frequency affects your results, and the first way to do this is to know where you stand. Don't offend or get angry at yourself. If there is something you're not happy with when you did this exercise, you're reading this book because you are seeking the solution. We need to establish our present baseline so we can understand our path moving forward in this guide. If you struggled with accepting responsibility for your current situation(s) in the exercises above and perhaps found an external person or circumstance to blame, then you may not be ready to do the work necessary to make a change in your life right now. An Elusive Perspective is an introduction to awakening the true power you have over yourself and your reality. You will not be able to execute this if you harbor belief systems which strip you of your power by placing responsibility on *"external"* factors. In fact, decide to make a change right now and relieve yourself of all those beliefs and take ownership of yourself. If you weren't able to do the exercise because your mind shifted into a blame game state, you're the exact person this book was meant for.

There are many others who can dive deeper into this topic and cover more ground than we will in this introduction. I highly recommend the *Source Field Investigations* by David Wilcock. He can be a little verbose and long-winded in his writing, but he provides an insatiable number of notes and scientific references for concepts surrounding frequency and vibration. At the end of this book there will be a list of material I highly recommend you catch up on for more in-depth information on everything we're covering here.

The Biology of Belief

I'm going to hit you guys with a doozy now. This is actually a very complex subject but I'm going

An Elusive Perspective

to give you the cliff notes and you can take it from here with your own study on the topic. Remember we're still covering foundations here and I would be negligent if I didn't bring this up. I have to cover material from a very well-respected cellular biologist and spiritual leader, Dr. Bruce H. Lipton. He wrote the "*The Biology of Belief*" and in my humble opinion, should be a crucial part of everyone's awakening. Why? Because in a nutshell it spits in the face of all that we've been taught about our bodies, health and the power we have to heal ourselves with the mind. Dr. Lipton's information ties directly in with frequency and vibration and how we can attract wants and desires into our life experiences, but he takes it further when we use that ability to focus on our bodies at the cellular level. He goes into so much detail with how cells work and the chemistry within and he explains it in a way that anyone can understand.

Essentially, the cells that make up our bodies can be affected by our vibrations and frequencies. I think inherently we can all agree that this makes sense. A healthy mind generally means a healthy body and spirit. The caveat here, according to Dr. Lipton, is we can focus on any health ailments we suffer from with the intent that it is healed (present tense), and the cells will react accordingly. We already know and have this phenomenon documented with the placebo effect. The placebo effect is an occurrence in the medical research community where patients are given medication, told what it is and what it is for, but in (objective) reality, it's usually just a sugar pill. Since the patient was lied to, they believe the medication will do what they were told and despite this being false, their bodies react as if they actually did receive the medication.

Our modern science has basically dismissed the placebo effect as a fluke we don't quite understand and is not worth studying or mentioning further than a few minutes in medical schools. Let's be honest, there is no money in medicine if it is understood that the mind has the ability to cure and/or directly reverse most if not all health issues. The medical industry believes the placebo effect is significant enough for an honorable mention but nothing more outside of that. Dr. Lipton believes this proves that our minds can actually heal our bodies with the power of belief. The placebo effect proves this, but our mainstream Doctors and science absolutely refuse to go any further into it, and why would they? It does nothing for their bottom line.

Let me be completely honest here. I have a personal gripe with the medical industry and big pharma but allow me to provide flowers where they are due. I know there are scientists, doctors and nurses out there that actually care about people in general. Modern medicine does have its positives and there is a lot that we have accomplished as a society medically that we just were not doing decades or even centuries ago. I understand during COVID a lot of contempt was placed upon the medical profession, perhaps some warranted and some not. As Dr. Lipton has suggested, our modern medicine is great with trauma-related injuries such as surgeries and removing things or replacing them. However, when it comes to chemical or other biological illnesses such as viruses and non-trauma related diseases, our modern medicine fails us remarkably. Ultimately it is not all the practitioners' fault. The medical academic institutions are to blame because they obviously do not have the best interest of the people at heart (pun intended).

There is another phenomenon which mirrors the placebo effect called the nocebo effect. It is the opposite of the placebo effect in that something which would not ordinarily cause a person harm, does, simply because the person believes it will. You would think the placebo and nocebo effects would warrant much more mainstream research and study to fully develop some applications that the public could use, but I digress. The major takeaway here should be that there is an avenue of self-health care, and it begins with us and within our mind. Imagine the financial hemorrhaging of the pharmaceutical industry if word got out that we actually don't need chemicals and harmful, side effect laden drugs that cost us billions per year.

In his book, Dr. Lipton shows us the many different ways that we can heal ourselves with the power of intention and belief. Biologically, each of us is a community of 50 trillion individual cells; and the mind is the government of those 50 trillion entities. Each one of our cells has their own organs which function to keep the cell alive, just as we do. As above, so below (keep this in mind). Each cell of our body is one of the whole, as we are one of the whole of our society. Each cell has a consciousness, and we can affect our cells with intention and belief to overcome illness and disease. We must have conviction in our belief that our bodies can overcome anything. Think about what we've been taught about DNA and the human genome. They've told us over and over that DNA cannot change. They ask us our family medical history and stamp us as casualties of previous family diagnoses. We are taught that we have no control over our own bodies and to just be victims of genetic determinism. I understand there is a level of genetic inheritance that passes down, but they always made it seem as if that's where the buck stops. There is always the individual and the mind that has the last say, always.

It is my belief that our conscious minds are that higher intelligence to our biological cells in the same way that The Universe is our higher intelligence. As above so below. There is a design and fractal pattern to everything in existence. If Dr. Lipton's theory is correct (and I believe it is) then we ultimately have dominion over the cells in our body and our own health from a biophysics perspective. Of course, there is exercise and eating appropriately and the plethora of things we all know to do when it comes to physical health. The same way we can manifest our reality from within our minds, we can manifest health and longevity. It's a two-way street and we as a collective should learn to master manifesting in both paths. I only bring you this information because I think it's imperative for you to hear it and be introduced to it. Most of us have not and I believe this is a travesty. Please look further into Dr. Lipton's work and explore the implications of what he's saying.

Can I Pet That Wabbit?

ILLUSIVE ILLUSIONS

Can I Pet That Wabbit?

2

You've Been Asleep, Neo

Hopefully in *Foundations*, you've learned some new things, but now, it is time for the unlearning. We will begin to shed some light on common falsities that most of us were taught at a very early age. Most of us carry these early beliefs throughout life, sometimes even all the way to death. We must work on unlearning mistruths about reality and what most of us would call "common knowledge" today. If you think long and hard enough, you can remember at some point in your young life being told something that maybe didn't sound right or that didn't resonate to you despite your age. At the time, you may have felt strange about the information you were given, but then shrugged it off because it came from an "all-knowing" adult; or better yet, a "book" obviously written by a grown-up, because if you're five years old and it's in a book, how could it be wrong?

Children are both very intuitive and to their own detriment extremely impressionable. As children we can believe in fairy tales and invisible friends while also having an innate sense of natural intelligence about us. Unfortunately, this matrix that we are all born into has a way of snuffing out that intuition and installing its own programming, for its own benefit. Some of us throughout life find a way to awaken and identify these falsities, but then others can grasp onto them for an entire lifetime and suffer greatly because of it. Once you are awakened, you can then identify what I call an "Illusive Illusion". An illusive illusion is:

"A belief which oppresses or deceives its believers."

To be clear, an illusive illusion is *NOT* the lie itself, we have other words for that such as propaganda. An illusive illusion can only be identified by those not victim to the false belief. If you are one of the believers, you can't identify it (yet).

The American political system has an astounding compilation of Illusive Illusions reeking from both political parties. Some would probably prefer to reduce my definition of an illusive illusion down to just being an opinion, but that would be incorrect. An opinion is held on a personal level and yes, many people can have the same opinions, but opinions don't necessarily have to be oppressive, deceptive or even wrong for that matter. There is much more weight to the mass deception under this term. Also, an illusive illusion must be a belief adopted by a large number of people. And that large number of people must specifically be negatively affected by holding this belief. The opinion of a person liking or not liking a movie holds no weight on that person's well-being; however, being of the belief that a certain group of people hate you and therefore you must hate them is a major illusive illusion most people suffer from (much more on this later).

A perfect example of an illusive illusion that unfortunately a vast number of people still share today is the idea that diet sodas are better for you than non-diet. In fact, not only do diet sodas NOT help anyone lose weight, but in some instances, they may be more damaging to your health than getting the regular non-diet drink. Our food industry also has an astounding number of illusive illusions that millions of people believe. The matrix and food industry, specifically, has had decades to perfect its marketing ploys against the public and steer us toward "health" or "diet" alternatives which do everything but provide us health or nutrition. We're going to get into this and other deeper illusive illusions, but I first wanted to drive home what an illusive illusion is.

An unfortunate truth of awakening is that it's impossible to go back to sleep. At that point, you simply know too much and going back to the old paradigm is not an option. That nail in your mind will never disappear and so technically you will never be the same. Later, we'll discuss some ways of dealing with this nail in your mind without going completely bat shit. But for now, let's focus on some of the more common illusive illusions out there and see if you can resonate with the truth. Remember, you have the choice to reject all of this. In essence this is still your red pill, blue pill moment. It's a possibility you may resonate with some but not all of these illusive illusions and that's fine as well. The actual goal here is to open your mind to possibilities that you otherwise would've never had the opportunity to entertain. Don't forget, this is just an introduction to waking the fuck up. I'll try to refrain from hitting you with the more complex substance for now. The deeper material will be introduced in later editions of this book series.

3
The Illusion of Scarcity

The Illusion of Scarcity

Prepare yourself, because the true triggering will commence now. There is no such thing as scarcity or lack thereof. You've been lied to your whole entire life. There has always been more than enough to go around. This is my favorite illusive illusion because once I was able to fully grasp it, I was never the same, and hopefully this will be true for you as well. From the day we can conceive thoughts and ideas, the matrix does everything in its power to convince us that we live in a world of lack and scarce resources. You've probably heard "Money doesn't grow on trees" five times a day as a child when you asked for something. "There's not enough to go around" was probably your parents' motto once or twice a week. In our media, books, movies, and music, we are bombarded with narratives of poverty and struggle and confirmations that "this is just the way it is and always has been." Our social media is littered with people complaining about inflation and financial struggles all the time. Our news constantly assaults us with propaganda of financial, energy and oil crises. Almost every bit of information flowing through our media is tuned into a message of poverty, lack, struggle, and scarcity.

Every four years our politicians promise us they can make things better if we just vote for them and every four years, they are all still very much discussing the same problems. Ask yourself, why is this so? Who sets this precedent? Are the world's resources really that scarce? Shouldn't the people *in charge* have been smart enough to have solved these problems by now? How are we in the 21st century with centuries and millennia of combined human experience and yet poverty and struggle is still a thing we have yet to conquer as a society? These are all great questions. In case you've never heard this

The Illusion of Scarcity

point of view before, please allow me to be the first to tell you with 100% certainty and the utmost and highest confidence that not only is there enough to go around for everyone, but that this idea of worldwide scarcity is a completely fabricated and intentional illusion crafted with the sole purpose of keeping you in a state of fear, low vibration and a mindset of "just fuck it."

Sit and think about this for just a while. Throughout most of our recorded human history, the people in charge have not solved the poverty and resource problems. This isn't because it's such a hard "problem" to solve, it's because their actual role is to facilitate the illusion and keep it thriving. We've had poverty and slaves since the Ancient Egyptian and Roman days and to this day we still have poverty and slaves, and the world tells us this is the way it is. I call bullshit.

Mine, and your job now is to dismantle these illusions one by one. If all of us, as a society understand these illusive illusions and break them down and unlearn them, the collective consciousness of this planet will improve tremendously and exponentially. It would have no choice but to. These are the lies we have been believing in all our lives and explains the circumstances we've been attracting for ourselves. The matrix needs believers in its illusions, that's the only way they can hack into our subjective realities to help manifest *their* goals. The matrix is so desperate for active participants it targets us in our most vulnerable state, children.

Natural Law Proves Abundance

"What do you mean there's enough to go around for everybody!? I grew up dirt poor, so I know for a fact poverty is real! You don't have a clue what you're talking about!"

The Illusion of Scarcity

I knew you'd say that. Allow me to explain. As discussed previously, we must defer to the natural laws of our universe. Nature literally shows us that we live in abundance all around us! Again, objective reality reveals to us that just one apple seed can potentially produce thousands or even millions of potential future apples. And each one of those apples can produce an insane amount more. This one example here is quite literally all you need to know to understand that abundance is the true state of the natural world. Everything exists in fractals of each other. That means everything in existence is created from something else already in existence. An infinite loop of creation so to speak. Abundance is written into the core fabric of objective reality! It works without question and without fail and does not need our recognition! (I'm yelling a lot so let me calm down a bit.) That one apple tree can produce hundreds or even thousands of apples in one season. Imagine the food resource for all the neighboring wildlife. And that's just one apple tree. Earth provides us with berries, acorns, nuts, vegetables and so on. This is just one example of the abundance of food resources on the planet. I'm illustrating here potentiality. Yes, farming and agriculture is no easy feat and there's many things to consider for successful crops on a mass scale. Without getting too deep into the complexities of farming to scale for the population, we *know* that nature provides us seeds that can grow food. One seed of any fruit or vegetable has the potential to feed hundreds of people. How can we NOT see that abundance is written into the fabric of objective reality?

Think of the vast amounts of land on Earth. The plains, the hills. Acres and acres of fertile soil. Think of your own backyard (if you have one). What do you have planted out there? What could you plant out there if you knew how to garden properly? The American dream told us to buy a house, grow lush green grass and rake leaves off our lawns. We run to supermarkets to buy poisoned and processed food (more on this later). Meanwhile, the true food resource potential is literally the entirety of the Earth.

Have you ever taken a long road trip and marveled at the vast number of trees and empty land that is out there? How much untapped soil? We can fit every living human being on Earth into the state of Texas with a half an acre of land each. There are about 200 countries in the world and all the people of each of those countries can live inside of Texas. What does this imply to you? This tells us that we are vastly spread out across the Earth and there is abundant land for everyone to live extremely comfortably. But of course, if you live in one of the 10,000 densely populated cities in the world you probably wouldn't know that or even had an opportunity to experience otherwise. A lot of us live on top of each other in overpopulated project buildings and municipalities where we're crammed up like cattle. When it comes to physical living space the matrix quickly convinces us this "lack" is normal. The Earth provides us with all the necessary food and land we need to thrive. It is the powers that be and the matrix that sell you overpriced processed food, cram you into dense cities with extortionate housing, and pull the wool over your eyes to the truth of the true abundance in this reality.

The only reason we even have these ideas of scarcity and lack in our society is because of what we are told and what is enforced through the matrix. There are controls in place which impose these ideas onto us. They go out of the way to ensure most of us are born into these dense cities where struggle is the norm. You'll notice I might keep going back to what we were taught as children as a prime example of the programming agenda, but it's true. It's much easier to program agendas into a child than an adult who may have more critical thinking ability. Our parents were also once children indoctrinated with the same teachings, and their parents before them. To be brutally honest, food, water and land are three of the most abundant resources on this planet. These three things are provided to all of us naturally and abundantly. The matrix has seized distribution of these resources, hoarded them, put a hefty price tag and bombarded us with experiences and stories of poverty and struggle. But despite knowing that, we are all very much still in control if we focus on the vibration and reality we wish to experience. All their control and oppressive devices still operate under the laws of subjective reality, which means they fall under the same rules as everything else. You can operate on a frequency where their control and oppressive devices cannot exist in your reality! Some people already do this, unfortunately most of us do not. If most of Earth's inhabitants pick up this way of thinking, the matrix and its controls will not have any power to continue to project these illusive illusions. It really is as simple as awakening from the nightmare.

An Elusive Perspective

Money Follows the Rules Too

"What about money!?

The first thing people need to understand about money is that it is nothing more than a tool invented by the matrix to convert what is naturally available to us into an exchangeable medium. What I mean is the matrix needed a means to monetize natural resources for control. And while we can understand this, we also must understand that it too, must abide by the laws of nature in that same respect. Everything in this plane of existence abides by these rules. If it exists in this realm and you can touch it and feel it with your physical hands, it is bound to these rules, whether it is a tool of the matrix or not. This means like the apple, there is an abundance of money in the world, for everyone to enjoy, utilize and thrive on. So, what is the problem? Well, like the illusions created around food and land, the powers that be also perpetuate the illusion of a lack of financial resources. There are many ways to debunk this illusion. Before we can debunk, we need to understand how the illusion is maintained and of course nurtured into our subjective realities.

As previously mentioned, children are most susceptible to influence and belief systems when they are very young. Most of us were not raised in wealthy or financially comfortable families (shocker). As we grew up our parents constantly reminded us of how broke we were and why we couldn't get the things we wanted and naturally, children want a lot of things when we're young. At those ages we have not yet been exposed to the matrix concepts of "supply and demand" or "exchanging time for money." Our parents most likely felt this way about money because of their circumstance and because their parents before them spoke of and thought about money in the same way. This repetitive idea of "money being hard to obtain" is a program from the matrix installed that has been on autopilot for many generations. This is primarily how the system deceives us into being on the vibration and frequency of "money struggles." We broadcast out into the Universe this vibration and receive it back. Most of the matrix's programming is completed when we are very young, and we auto execute the belief throughout our lives. Of course, this is not the entire reason most of us are born into lack and struggle. You have to understand, the mind control is a huge part of maintaining the illusive illusion, but it's not the whole cannoli. Just as with food and land, the matrix imposes controls which support the idea of the lack of financial resources. And when we experience these controls, we tend to lean towards the self-confirmation bias of the illusion. And thus, the feedback loop executes, and our mindset combined with their controls manifests more and more poverty into our lives.

The Illusion of Scarcity

Something to think about and try with your children if you have them. Don't *EVER* tell your children you're broke. Don't enforce to them they can't get something because you don't have the money. Don't instill in them the idea of scarcity and lack. We can all break the cycles now. I rarely speak to my son negatively about our family's financial situation for this very reason. If you ask him, he thinks we're rich. Plot twist: we *ARE* (see what I did there, we're not, (but are we?) Bitch, we might be). Anyway, we speak only abundance and prosperity in our household. I've never told my son we can't get something because I couldn't afford it, and if I have it was very early on before I learned what I'm speaking of now. Keep in mind, I'm not saying be deceptive to your children. I'm saying be more aware of the words you use when speaking to them. They carry tremendous weight, and you shouldn't speak into the Universe a reality you don't wish to experience (especially if you are). As an example, if your child asks for something, instead of "No, because I can't afford that", a simple "No" can suffice without attachment to something like lack of resources or money. Another very important thing to stop doing is speaking negatively, especially in regard to health. Never say "I am sick," even if you are unwell for whatever reason, say "I am healing." Speak prosperity into all your situations. In terms of financial hardship, never ever give power to the unwanted circumstance with affirmative words and thoughts. This only provides validation to the Universe and brings more reality validation to your experience. Words are extremely important, whether written, spoken, or thought. It is imperative that you understand the importance of your word choice when speaking into situations, writing about them or thinking about them. We cover much more in depth in *Chapter Seven: Manifesting* as it pertains to money and other things.

Outside of our upbringings, the matrix perpetuates the idea of financial scarcity by constant negative news about our economy and the national

The Illusion of Scarcity

debt. There was in fact a time where I cared about our growing national debt, so much that it felt it was my own personal debt, and it affected me negatively in my life. I honestly was never sure why I allowed national debt news to affect me. I just knew it was bad for our country and if the media was making it a big deal, that I should be thinking about it as well. The agenda here was to make us feel bad about the country's financial situation and in doing so, manifest continuing financial stresses in our own lives. I mean, if the country can't get it together why do we think we could be any better? Well, it's a good thing the national debt doesn't affect us individually, in fact, it never did. Turn off the news. If you ask an economist, they will certainly begin to explain to you how and why you should care. Respectfully, fuck 'em. Let economists worry about the national debt. You have resources to manifest for yourself and your situation.

In addition to just plain ol' negativity in the media, we must also address the obvious matrix

An Elusive Perspective

devices that were designed to suppress our ability to earn and facilitate the scarcity theory. The matrix public education system does indeed shepherd us towards a lifelong commitment of servitude through trading time for labor. There is no doubt about this. The second Industrial Revolution of the 1900's ushered in the 9-5, 40-hour work week schedule. It's been over 100 years since this travesty was bestowed upon us. We as a society have been on autopilot for so long trading time for money and most of us continue to this day playing this rat race game. We have seen such a growing disparity between the highest paid personnel of a major corporation to the lowest paid and that disparity has become immense over the decades. Again, as I stated before, this is not by chance but by matrix design. There are options to opt out of this system. Of course, going into business for yourself is a means of escaping the employee rat race. And naturally, there are pros and cons to that, but this is not a business book, so we aren't going into details on becoming an entrepreneur in this book. Perhaps that will be a topic for a future edition of "An Elusive Perspective".

The point is there are many ways to make money outside of the 40-hour work week employee purgatory the matrix has conveniently laid out for us. Sidenote: if you have a 9-5 job and actually like your job and pay rate, please disregard any negative tones and bias I am showing. Your work choice experience is valid and if it truly makes you happy then it is perfect for you! This just means you do not weigh money as a primary source for your happiness and that is perfectly ok. Once you understand that money is not as "elusive" as it is made out to be you will be shocked to see how much begins to start flowing into your life.

We All Don't Want the Same Things

Some of us have very specific and unique dreams. Others may have more common dreams. When it comes to the abundance of this realm, not everyone wants the same things. It is very possible to live a healthy, long and relationship abundant life where money is *not* the focal point. The Universe has a sense of humor in that way where it can literally make a way for any possibility. Perhaps you are such an individual that does not prioritize or weigh finances as an indicating factor of happiness or success in your life. That is 100% perfectly fine. It is this balance that allows others to desire and pursue the things you are not; and vice versa. If every human on this planet were all the same, with the same exact desires across the board, what a boring place this would be. The Universe has provided a realm of abundance through diversity as well as sheer numbers. We are taken care of! We just have to know we are and let the Universe know we are! Any amount of doubt in your mind will bring forth to you a reality where the doubt in your dream will be present. If you believe everyone is after the same thing, you will co-create a world of scarcity. Arguably, due to our current society it may seem that a majority of us really do prioritize money as a determining indicator of happiness. Again, that is a matrix default program. A lot of us think we need financial abundance to be happy because the matrix says so. That is untrue.

I recently got into a debate with the co-hosts of one of my podcasts "Figuring Conspiracy Shxt Out" (search us on Rumble). I simply asked the question, what if there was no such thing as "work" and humans didn't need to work to earn money in order to pay for food, a dwelling and utilities? That was the question. There were no other caveats or assumptions or implications made. Simply, what if we didn't need to work for resources? I swear their minds exploded. Long story short, I don't think I could get them to imagine the possibility. We are so attached to this capitalist existence where a lot of us simply cannot imagine not requiring money to work or be productive. It boiled down to my co-hosts believing that without work or a job that there would be nothing to do, everyone would get fat and bored, chaos would ensue, and mankind would not be able to progress or dream at all. Me, however, all I could see was the possibilities open to spending every waking hour doing what I wanted to do and only what I wanted to do and not what I was obligated to do. Most of my activities in this perfect world would involve reading and writing books, producing music and spending time with family. That's just me. Others would probably have more ambitious goals or less ambitious endeavors. The point I'm making here is we are not all the same and want the same things. There is even enough diversity within human desires to accommodate all of us. Some of us want to be singers, farmers, athletes, pastors, artists, doctors, scientists, etc. Imagine if money wasn't a thing we were all required to live off of. Everyone would be doing those things irrespective of a "career" or a "job" they needed to survive. We wouldn't spend a third of our lives doing a thing we hated in order to pay bills. I get it, this sounds like a pipe dream, but I honestly don't think it's far from reality.

Ironically enough, there are people who live like this today. Just think about it. We have living amongst us, billionaires and millionaires who literally do what they want on a daily basis. They have the freedom so many of us seek. Of course, by being financially wealthy they are obviously plugged into the capitalist system and also dependent upon it as we are. Putting that aside, these people have achieved what many of us desire – true time freedom. So that's the first point, there are people living on Earth today, that have no worries about having to spend time in their day doing something they don't want to do. Don't focus on the fact these people are rich, the point is people are living worry free right now, which means it is a reality that you can tap into as well. It is on the menu of the Universe. On the flip side of this, there are people who live their lives not prioritizing money by choice. Jack Reacher is a fictional character in books and TV that travels about the world, saving the day, doing good deeds and solving crimes while having pennies to his name. I guess you can call him a Nomad of sorts. A Nomad is a person that travels about the world and doesn't own a home or permanent dwelling. They work odd jobs here and there to get around and are not tied down to any specific location. These are people who happily do not prioritize money or finances and make do with what they have no matter where they are. This is a choice, and they choose it because it makes them happy. The Nomadic lifestyle tends to reject owning property or being tied to one location due to where you live or work. These are two primary examples of how we all don't want or pursue the same things. The matrix has you believing that the world is full of scarcity because we are all the same and want the same things. We don't. The Universe shows us every day that there is enough of everything for everybody. It is the matrix which produces the illusions of scarcity. We all have a choice whether we want to choose money as a conduit to achieve our goals or reject it. The Universe will do its job either way to facilitate you if you know how to speak to it.

4

The Illusion of Depression

The Illusion of Depression

This was a hard chapter to write. Let me first state that in no way is this section implying that people have not or are not depressed presently or in the past. Remember, this book is about awakening, so there will be hard truths. I will not claim to have all the answers regarding the purpose of people suffering here on Earth. I am still a human being just like you. There are various beliefs on suffering such as soul contracts and Karma, but those concepts are really out of the scope of this book. Instead, we're going to keep it to a very simple level. I'm going to provide you with some tools to deal with situations where you may find yourself "depressed" and get out on the other side the best version of yourself. I'll also explain how depression is an illusive illusion induced

An Elusive Perspective

to the masses by the matrix and why you should reject this programming by all means necessary and with *full* intention.

First off, what is depression? Depression is emotional warning alerts from your mind, body and spirit or all three. It's a warning that something needs to change and fast. Our current medical "science" loves to provide their chemical fixes which do nothing more than alter the mind to numbness, so depression isn't "felt" as much. This does not address the core issue but is only a temporary mask as those drugs do absolutely nothing for healing the source of the emotional warning. In case you're not aware already, most of our current medical industry focuses on masking symptoms while keeping the core health issues in place. They want this because there is no money in cures, only prolonged treatments. So don't be surprised to learn that their depression solutions are nothing more than temporary expensive relief. Do not rely on the matrix controls of "diagnoses" and "prescriptions drugs" which the system tells you, you need to overcome depression. When the drug wears off, you're back at square one and back at the pharmacy refilling your prescription of numbness pills.

In a perfect world, a person who is experiencing feelings of depression would be alerted to the emotion and seek within to find the source and correct it, whatever that could be. He or She would focus on what the trigger was, what thoughts they might have had during the trigger and/or current events in their life that may have altered their state of mind. Once you understand the true source of an issue, only then can you seek the solution you need for correction. Today, there are so many reasons people may feel depressed and of course as I have already stated, the matrix was designed for optimizing negative and low vibrations in all of us. To be depressed today is to be *HERE* it seems. Executing the matrix's programming of "all the reasons to be depressed" is quite common. Money, bills, our relationships, our jobs. Remember, the

An Elusive Perspective

world has been programmed to work against you but only if you adhere to the programming.

Here's a tip when you feel "feelings" of depression. You must switch your idea of being in a "depressed" state to the idea of being in an "opportunity for discovery" state. What does this mean? Our emotions and how we feel provide us with much information about our current state. If you feel bad, or your emotions are in a low vibratory state, this is your sign something is wrong and to do something about it. Use the opportunity to discover what it is that is out of alignment in your mind, body, or soul. There are only two paths to take: correction or stagnation. And hear me when I say, both are choices. It does not matter if your idea of correction will take a long *time*. Make the *MOVES*. Do the *THINGS*. Begin the journey to *CORRECTION*. Anything else is Stagnation and therefore choosing to remain in your depressed state!

The Illusion of Depression

So, I say all that to say this: Depression is a choice. Yes, you read that correctly. Depression is your mind, body or soul telling you that you need to move. You are stagnant. Nature is in constant motion. So should you be. There are people who have clinical "diagnoses" of depression provided by their doctor and they will fight you tooth and nail to protect their status of "clinically depressed". Why is that a problem? Because you are advocating and fighting for your subjective reality to run the programming that you are depressed, and you are placing yourself under the delusion that you are helpless to do anything about it. That energy being placed into defending your "depressive" state can just as easily be used to overcome and climb out of such a state. Can it be hard? Of course it can. Raise your vibration and unlearn paradigms about yourself. Understand that your subjective reality that you were effortlessly executing is to be in a depressed state. How can I say this? Because you are "depressed". Recall our earlier discussion.

An Elusive Perspective

"I vibrate at the resonating frequency of depression, because I am depressed".

Wake Up from this! *MOVE!* Let me cut to the chase. This is how I approach an unfavorable situation which may lead to feelings of depression. I promise this is 1,000% better than going into straight panic, chaos or stagnation mode. No matter what it is, I stop and assess what has happened *FIRST*. Take a pause and ingest your feelings. Ask yourself, is this really a problem and if it is, how much of a problem is it? Within these two questions you may be surprised to find answers come to you quickly. The mind has an amazing way of identifying solutions if we stop and pause to assess calmly.

One of my struggles and I'm sure most could relate was my issue with money, the lack of resources and the struggle to pay bills and weigh priorities as far as what I can pay now, what I can pay later and what I can take a late penalty on. A typical occurrence amongst the populace. I remember allowing these feelings of lack to really get under my skin and I dare say it, to the point of a type of depression. Remember, depression is an emotional warning. Me not having enough money to do what I needed to, let alone live how I wanted was weighing in on me. It's not a good feeling, especially over a prolonged amount of time. So, what's the solution? Stop worrying! I had to tell myself, actively and frequently that despite my "reality" in finances that I am in control of my life, and I can turn this situation around just as much as I found myself in it! The depressed mind sees no way out because it has given up! Do Not Give Up! Festering and dwelling in negative and low vibrational states tells the Universe to provide you with more situations in which you can continue to fester and dwell. They say worrying is fear of the future and it is absolutely true.

I have done this many times in my life and in an instant felt the gratification and weight lift off my shoulders and spirit. I understand, most people would take this advice as just "ignore" all of your problems. My response to that is no; never ignore your problems, that's not what I'm saying at all. Take solace in that despite having problems, your mindset is the one ultimate champion you have to find a solution and climb out of whatever issue you are currently facing. If you find yourself in a perpetual state of depression, assess yourself, find the core problem where your depression is stemming from and begin a plan to overturn it. If it's money, that can be fixed. If it's debt, that can be paid. If it's your weight, that can be brought down. If it's relationships with others, work on yourself. If it's health reasons, deep dive into holistic research for a solution. Lastly, there are some of those things that you simply do not have power or control over to change. We all have them. For those items, stop worrying about it! Focus on what you DO have control over.

Of course, seeking professional help should always be an option. I would never tell anyone not to seek help. I personally have trust issues with most medical professionals in general and I'm ok with admitting that, however, I know for a fact there are many well-meaning healthcare providers that are really out there fighting the good fight and helping people. If you seek professional help, I advise you to pray to your God, or ask the Universe for guidance and assistance on finding the right provider for you that has your best interest at heart and is not just interested in writing prescriptions to fatten their pockets. I think if you use discernment and open yourself to auras and vibrations you will be able to detect someone's intentions and whether they will be a good fit for you. One quick tip when dealing with a healthcare provider (or anyone for that matter) is if you personally feel you are being "sold" on a solution, then chances are pretty high that you are. Energy transfers, and if you are in tune with yourself, your intuition will alert you when dealing with someone who is disingenuous every time.

5

The Illusion of Information

The Illusion of Information

At the turn of the century, our civilization was just beginning to enter the information age, or probably better known now as the digital information age. We have at our fingertips the ability to access almost any tidbit of information available on the planet. There is a YouTube video to explain or show you how to do the simplest of things, from changing a tire to paying your taxes. News and media outlets scramble daily to put out the latest click-bait headlines and bring readers and advertising dollars in while cable and television studios do the absolute most to grab your attention.

I admit the title of this chapter may be a misnomer. Information cannot technically be an "illusion." All information to some extent is valid because it has a purpose. Generally speaking, it is the purpose of the information which comes into question. I wrote this chapter because I think it is important to understand that there is a greater percentage of information being provided to us daily that is increasingly agenda driven. What this means is that we are continuously bombarded with misleading and false headlines, with the purpose of our own self oppression, self-destruction, to incite hatred for others and to misinform us about who we really are. What I hope you take away from this chapter is an acknowledgement of this, regardless of any bias you may have towards any media outlets which you may believe to be trustworthy. I can certainly assure you, that the amount of information you take in daily from social media, major news outlets, radio, internet, schools, textbooks, or any other outlet, is unfortunately mostly false, misleading, or fabricated at the bare minimum. I'm sure there is reliable news and information out there. What I'm saying is we, as a society and as the consumers of this information, must be vigilant in what we hear and see. Almost to the point of a zero-trust relationship. Our own biases cannot protect us from the lies we want to hear, and of that there are plenty.

Our Food Is Poison

Yes, we shall take it there. I understand those four words may seem abrasive. Most of us already know this. If you don't know, you may have only heard it at least a few dozen times and brushed it off your shoulders because the food they keep saying this about tastes good and you really like it. That is why most of us keep eating the food we know is killing us. Oh, and let's not forget because it's cheap. That's the second reason. This is not a health book, remember, this is just an introduction and so we are touching on many different topics. If you want to get further, deeper information please do your own research or look out for the later editions of "An Elusive Perspective" as they are released. Here's the caveat though, all of us are 100% ultimately responsible for what we put into our bodies. Full stop. Even if we don't know how bad it is for us, "they" know it. When I say "they" I mean Big Food and Big Pharma. If you've never heard of Big Food or Big Pharma allow me to elaborate. Big Food are the conglomerate food corporations. These are the corporations which have the funding and Research & Development departments that make our food tasty but also extremely addictive. They do so in the name of profits, obviously. What better way to ensure repeat customers than to use the chemistry of the brain to make food addictive enough for us to keep coming back? It doesn't matter if the additives and chemicals put in our foods are bad for us because this is the alley-oop over to their stepbrother Big Pharma. Big Pharma comes in and prescribes us their patented chemical solutions which only ever address symptoms and never the root causes of disease. And let's not forget those chemical pills also have side-effects of their own which you will also need more pills for.

Cutting back to the chase. The USDA's food pyramid was complete and utter bullshit. Think about this, the food pyramid had the recommendation of 6-11 servings a day of bread, grain, cereal, rice or pasta. Today, through rigorous debunking and research, we now know that sugar heavy diets have mostly been the root cause of the explosion of chronic illness in our country. Not coincidentally, our bodies naturally produce sugar from carbohydrates. Think about it, our trusty USDA put out a recommendation of 6-11 servings of carbohydrate heavy foods, and America literally blew up for it. Although most health and nutrition experts know this today, our food industry still has not caught up to the idea that bread products in particular should not be in as much abundance in our food supply as they are. Americans still very much are consuming bread, grain, cereal, rice or pasta at alarming rates on top of sugary products like soda or fruit juices. I remember when I awakened to this reality and did my best to ween off the high carbohydrates, not only was it extremely difficult because I was an addict, but everywhere I looked bread was shoved in my face and made readily available at every turn. Our food culture still heavily promotes breakfast sandwiches, submarines, hamburgers, hot dogs, pancakes and more. The foods that taste so good and give us that full belly feeling we've come to crave. I remember when I'd have a meal without any type of bread and how empty I felt. My brain had literally asked me what else you got? This is when I knew I had an addiction. Something most of us wouldn't necessarily be ok with admitting. If you think about it, you, yourself probably eat some type of carb for each of the three meals per day. Do you? Most likely. Heavy carb diets are etched into our culture. Your parents and grandparents most likely also had a heavy carbohydrate diet. Your great-grandparents probably not so much. This push of a heavy carbohydrate diet can be clearly and concisely blamed on the food pyramid.

Go into any grocery store, food shopping mart or heck, just go to your pantry right now and pick up any food item in a packaged box or bag and look at the ingredients. Not the nutrition facts; the actual ingredients right below that. It is here in this ingredient list where they list the actual chemicals which causes over 60% of the chronic diseases to Americans. Perhaps you will be shocked to learn that some of the ingredients you will find here are banned in other countries. I wish I could tell you why America is this way. This is a special country and so we get special things that most other countries aren't necessarily dealing with all the time, such as racism (more on this later). Ingredients such as titanium dioxide, potassium, bromate, or brominated vegetable oil are ok for Americans but not for Europe for instance. But it's not only the banned ingredients that are bad for you. Canola oil, vegetable oil, high fructose corn syrup, natural flavors, added sugars and

An Elusive Perspective

others. On full display, right before your eyes, in our processed foods are the ingredients that are killing us. In black and white. Now that you know this, you must do better. I recommend a book by Dr. Livingood called *"Livingood Daily: Your 21-Day Guide to Experience Real Health."* In this book Dr. Livingood breaks down in many more details the woes of our processed food industry, the ingredients to stay away from and how to eat to live as opposed to living to eat.

If they are poisoning us with the food, why would they put it right there on the package? I'm glad you asked. The simple answer is they know most of us will still buy it anyway. Remember the matrix has a job of providing false choice under the guise of freedom. Have you ever wondered why "health" foods seem to be much more expensive than the regular foods we consume daily? It's no wonder to see there is an agenda to push us towards certain foods and steer away from others altogether. This is not by accident. But don't be fooled, even a lot of "health" foods which are marketed as such, are not as innocent as they seem. There is a general rule when it comes to truly finding healthy food, and I'll tell it to you right now. Any food that is as close to its original form as when it came from the Earth is best for you. The only caveat with this statement is for any meat product, the animal must also have been consuming natural foods from the Earth as well. A lot of the meat we consumed has been poisoned with unhealthy diets, antibiotics and other chemicals provided to the animal during its life. Those unhealthy things are then passed onto us via the meat. For example, when it comes to beef, do your best to buy "grass-fed" beef products. Anything not labeled as grass-fed is most likely fed grain which we have learned is not good in larger consumptions and also, not good for the cows themselves. Cows that are fed grain develop digestive issues that throw off their bacteria levels, and that leads to farmers having to pump up their sick cattle with antibodies. Seems like it doesn't matter what species of animal you are.

An Elusive Perspective

When you don't eat what your body was meant to, it causes problems and imbalances.

Use this section as a springboard to doing your own research on how the food industry has been damaging all of us for decades now. Take the time, get to know what foods harm and what foods help. There is a plethora of resources out there and people who know much better than me, that are trying to get the word out and educate us on the ways we should all be really eating. Start with Dr. Livingood and watch how eliminating certain foods can drastically change your life. After taking a course from Dr. Livingood and reading his book, I lost 20 lbs in a month from eliminating certain oils and paying attention to ingredients lists, and that was without exercise. The time to blindly trust "health" products and clever marketing tactics is over. If you want to extend your life and live with more energy daily, I suggest you get started right now.

American Politics

Most of the information we consume is false. I'm talking about industries in science, medicine, current events, politics, finance, history and the list goes on. We are being lied too about almost everything. The best example I can use to illustrate this is American politics. This will not be an endorsement of any political party. I am actively condemning them both. Why? Because both major parties (and even the smaller ones) all fabricate information and/or promote falsities to push their own agendas. This crosses over into activist organizations as well. I will not endorse a political party over the other and confirm any readers' bias, and I'm not sorry to disappoint. I hope you are reading this chapter and entertaining a new paradigm of reality into your psyche. What I learned on my journey studying the political system is that there is one agenda above all else and that is the separation of all people. It is a system that pits man against woman, rich against poor, black against white, straight against gay, traditionalism against progressivism and so on.

Several years ago, I was extremely political. My social media timelines were full of reposts and retweets of major news articles and headlines. All of which elicited low vibration emotions from me and most likely those who shared my views. It was a constant barrage of negative and emotional headlines promoted to me and in turn I promoted them back out to my following. I'm not sure what came first, the algorithm efficiency or my near depressive state of mind due to the constant bombardment of negative news happening throughout the world. Robberies, murders, injustices, political drama, active shooters, war. My entire worldview was completely carved by major headlines. My own personal life didn't even seem a factor. I was too concerned with what the media was telling me I had to be angry about, and it

The Illusion of Information

worked quite well at eliciting an emotional response from me. At my breaking point, and after complete numbness, I had to give up all consumption of local, world and breaking news. I blocked the major news outlets. Stopped going to their websites. Did my best to not come across their headlines on my feeds. If I saw a headline, I scrolled immediately past it. If someone shared a post on my timeline, I rejected it. The relief was immediate, and the break allowed me to find myself and begin to focus on my own life and goals.

Later, when I made an attempt to re-enter "informed" society and "educate" myself about the world again, I was able to instantly realize when a headline had emotional and low vibrational tones attached to it. I also started to second guess what I was being told and questioned it; Something I never did before. The old me took in information from "reputable sources" as fact, every time. This new *me*, had something slightly different in mind. I started to raise an eyebrow at most of the information I received. And I also opened myself up to other news sources of information that the previous me could never dream of entertaining. I didn't do it because I was "switching up", I believe this was part of a natural thirst for a subjective reality that wasn't so skewed and emotional. Of course, a lot of the new information I came across I didn't agree with either, it wasn't in my paradigm or bias. But I still considered it. Over time, I began to see things differently, and instead of consuming only one perspective of information, I was now receiving and analyzing two main perspectives even when they were in direct conflict with one another. I honestly believe doing this allowed me to widen my perspective on the world and see things from opposing views and having the choice to choose between them or, the third option which I don't believe many of us even know we are capable of, which is deciding on rejection of both proposed ideologies. Sometimes when faced with only a binary choice, there is that third "Elusive Perspective" that tends to reflect objective truth more accurately. I would argue the truth between both political parties is either in between their narratives or completely outside of it.

After I became more aware of perspectives from people of a different background than me politically, I developed a theory on the true nature of political parties (which I briefly touched on previously). That theory is that the powers that be, developed this system in order to keep groups of people divided and hateful of each other. When you take a step back and look at it from that elusive perspective, it's quite marvelous, just how successful it has become. In this country, and in so many others, there are generally two main political groups to which most voters are forced to subscribe to. Each of these groups generally have a stance on any given topic or controversial subject. Do you find it odd that these two groups almost always have an opposing viewpoint from each other? Why is that? Depending on your subscription, you are more likely to agree with most of the ideologies that have already been defined in your political box. What this means is by default and by your own party affiliation, you oppose the rival party and almost all their values. This literally has been done for you just by the party you aligned yourself with (or your parents aligned you with). Generally, when you go to vote, you vote for your party, not the individual. I bet most of you reading this now that vote, vote for your political party up and down the tickets and have no clue who these people are. I know I did.

Here's why politics as a binary system is flawed. If your opposing political party comes up with an idea that may be useful for the general public or god forbid make sense, your own party's leadership has no choice but to counter it at all costs, because it's in the script. If your party proposes a bill that can help the general public, you will most certainly hear counter arguments from your rival party. I honestly believe this system is why solutions that better society can almost never be properly utilized and implemented. I won't even touch on how the balance of political power seems to bounce back and forth over the election cycles.

There are some ideas that neither party endorse nor even want to. This is how those ideas never get a seat at the table because they aren't represented in the binary system that is our political structure. All I am doing is illustrating how information we receive from our political affiliations is really just used to separate and divide the people. Why do we call the ideologies "The Left" or "The Right?" This notion by itself implies a separateness built within every conceivable idea. Don't get me wrong, being represented is important and there are indeed times when a single politician from either party can come forward with great ideas and seem like a true inspiration. Individuals can be great influencers and inspirers, however the political system they attach themselves to has a design and purpose and it functions quite well. Of course, this perspective can only be achieved by taking a step

An Elusive Perspective

back and looking from the outside. I challenge you to stop and think of your political affiliation and/or ideas and ponder how perhaps for most of your adult political life, you were always told it was the rival party that caused all the issues. If only they would see things *OUR* way. This is the separation mindset the system installs in all of us. "The issue isn't with us, we're the righteous and moral people, it's *THEM* that are messing everything up! If they could only see the errors in their ways, the entire world would be much better!" Guess what's being told on the other side? The exact same thing. I feel like I may be getting away from the point of this chapter. The point of all this political talk is that information you may be receiving from your chosen political party is highly intended to cause a rift between other people who you may actually have more in common than you realize. Also, to open your mind to more information that you wouldn't generally entertain to grasp a broader perspective of the world around you.

When I began entertaining the perspectives of the political party I wasn't raised in, I didn't see them as the enemy anymore. I started to sympathize and see viewpoints that humanized them. As I stated, I didn't agree with everything. It wasn't a flip of the switch. But I did learn and expand my mind to new thoughts and ideas about society that I could've never learned about in my previously narrow perspective.

Propagandist Narratives

Here is another example of how different information can be used for the same nefarious purpose of division and fear tactics. As I break this down, do your best to sit outside of any emotional response and look at this example from a top-down perspective. Toss away any biases or beliefs you have of the next subject. I'm going to describe two perspectives that took place at the same time and go over how different narratives and information were spread to cause rifts between friends and family.

At the height of the pandemic, there were generally two groups of people. Those who were for the COVID vaccine and those who were not. If you were for the vaccine, you believed that mainstream media and medical institutions had your best intentions at heart. You believed the vaccine would prevent COVID and stop the transmission. That was your reality, that was your paradigm, and you received relentless confirmation biases from the media, social media, radio, advertising, and federal and local government. You were also advised, directly or indirectly by those same outlets to stay away from, or distance yourself from, the anti-vaxxers who were selfish and only cared about themselves and their "freedoms." Even to the point of cutting off close family and friends for the holidays because of the dangers those people posed towards you and other vaccinated people. You were even convinced to not attend or hold funerals for your loved ones due to the ongoing threat of COVID. I will call these people "paradigm one."

Then there is "paradigm two." This group never trusted the vaccine to begin with and never trusted the media, the news and the health professionals and sources that pushed it. They most certainly didn't appreciate the public ostracism and threats of employment eligibility, or not being allowed to visit places such as restaurants and public buildings without proof of vaccination. They didn't believe the vaccine was safe and were not open to taking the risk. These people risked traveling with fake vaccination cards just to get around. They risked losing their jobs. They risked many freedoms that until those days were taken for granted in America by all. The media constantly berated them as hateful and selfish people.

Not too long after the mandates and large numbers of vaccinations, information began to spread of a "spike protein" that was rumored to be contagious and "infect" the unvaccinated for just being in proximity to a vaccinated person. This "spike protein" could essentially vaccinate an unwilling participant without their knowledge. This was characterized as a nefarious and intentional side-effect of the vaccine. People in "paradigm two" were warned to stay away from vaccinated people or else the "spike proteins" can get onto you and infect you with the vaccine. The "spike protein" information was circulated by alternative news media sources, insiders and credentialed Doctors and specialists. Remember this group didn't trust mainstream media, so their main source of information was what some would consider underground and/or conspiracy theory outlets. Nevertheless, it was their source, and they trusted and believed in it.

I can imagine you fit into one of these two described paradigms. But my challenge to you is not to agree or disagree with any paradigm or to seek endorsement for either one from me; that's not what

The Illusion of Information

we're doing here. Instead, step outside of yourself and look from an outsider perspective and find the commonality of what was happening here. Both paradigms received conflicting information, both paradigms trusted their sources, and both paradigms were instructed to avoid and distance themselves from the other group via a fear mechanism of "you will get infected." It was complete and utter chaotic division and so many of us fell straight for it. I can tell you my personal experience seeing this unfold. And I'm not here to boost my own ego or toot my own horn. I was never a part of "paradigm one." I never trusted what was being said and I chose to reject the vaccination. However, when news spread of a "spike protein," and people were told to stay away from the vaccinated at all costs. My mind immediately sprung into side eye mode, and I had to reject the notion of a contagious "spike protein." To me, it was too obvious what was happening here. More division. Another tactic to make people actively separate themselves from others who think

An Elusive Perspective

differently from them. It was the same play with a different narrative, and I just couldn't buy into it. My own self-awareness laughed at the idea of both sides now separating themselves from each other for fear of infection for totally different reasons. I am not here to endorse any of the subjective realities mentioned above. Although I have my own personal feelings, I am not here to tell you what to think about those two paradigms. I cannot corroborate anything about a contagious "spike protein," or the contents or nefarious agenda behind the vaccines. We each are here to decipher that for ourselves through our own subjective mechanisms and manifestations. What I am here to do however, is to provide you with the tools to understand more than just one side and again, choose that Elusive Perspective that may not be as obvious. I did not distance myself from my loved ones who were vaccinated, and they did not distance themselves from me. I am blessed to have been born in a family where our love and ties are more powerful than simple propaganda on the news and for that I am thankful. Not all people were blessed with this unfortunately.

At the time of this writing, there was a major election going on in the United States. Naturally, both major parties are conducting their normal operations of fear-based propagandist narratives and division. It does not matter where you stand, or who you perceive to be the morally superior party or candidate. You are being lied to in some form or fashion. That's the game. Accept it. Some of the lies sound so good to you that you cannot imagine the truth. You may even have convinced yourself that the other side is truly the party of evil and deception and your party is of light and love. Here is the real truth about the parties. Both are filled with amazing people who have passions, values and want what's best for themselves and their families. Both contain good and bad people. Both contain highly educated and highly misinformed people. And both are under misguided and propagandist narratives that skew their world views. A truly awakened person knows this. Now,

An Elusive Perspective

I'm not saying you shouldn't participate in elections. At the end of the day there is a choice to be made, however, I wish more people went into the election booths understanding that you are not voting against evil people. Choose the candidate that seems to have your best interests in mind. When you vote against a candidate or party under the guise of "they are evil people that want to destroy the country," you are not choosing yourself and abundance, you are choosing a false narrative that does not exist. Think back on how the controversy surrounding the COVID vaccine had both sides choosing to stay away from the other due to some impending "doom." Look how the narratives worked against each other but for the same purpose. When you are voting because you think the other side is immoral, or evil, you are accepting the same fate.

How can you discern the agendas behind the different types of information we receive daily? Why should you even care? Well, I think the reason is if you don't want to be used as a tool of hate and division then you may want to learn how to decipher information for what its true purpose is. This will take some exercise of course and I can't claim to know the agenda and purpose behind every piece of information that comes across on our news feeds. We will always have a choice, to accept, reject or construct other viewpoints based on data we receive. It is my honest belief that if you have the intention of not being deceived by the matrix and wish to operate in the higher vibrations, you will be gifted with awareness and understanding that will guide your insight. Ask the Universe to help you ingest information properly and decrease your chances of being steered towards an agenda that promotes lower vibrational frequencies. Here are just a few questions you can ask yourself when presented with a headline, a narrative or story you see or hear on the news.

What is the emotion being elicited from me with this information?

Is this piece of news attempting to make me view a specific demographic of people in a certain light? Is it a good light or bad light?

Is the source normally known to be fair or biased in reporting?

Does this headline seem to justify violence or hate towards a specific demographic?

Who benefits from this headline? Who doesn't? Why?

Asking yourself a range of questions similar to these can help you use discernment and approach information without a dark cloud of confusion over you. Of course, there are always different interpretations of answers to this, so don't try to focus too much on answering "correctly." The goal is to find yourself regularly assessing headlines instead of taking them as fact so you will begin to see a difference in how you perceive the news of the world.

The Illusion of Information

And this is the point. Stop taking all mainstream media as fact by default. It is far from it. Don't take alterative news sources as fact either, a lot of that is noise as well. If it's not flat out lies, they are skewed truths at best. For those of us who went to public school, you may remember the "current events" assignments where you had to find and pick a news article from a "reputable source" to report to the class. That "reputable source" was generally supposed to be from mainstream media. Why do you think they wanted us to only get our news from them? Think about it. If this is your first-time hearing about propaganda and misinformation in our very own trusted news sources, I could understand how this can be troublesome. But don't let it depress or discourage you from seeking truth.

The Land of Confusion

Here's a quick tip; Stay completely away from opinion pieces. I have had the misfortune of reading quite a few opinion pieces from established journalists and I must say some of the most destructive and irrational thoughts are literally splayed all over opinion pieces. For me, it wasn't even about disagreeing with the opinions per se, that's the easy part and not my issue; it was reading non-sensical, damaging and unreasonable rhetoric that the matrix clearly perpetuates. These days when I come across an opinion piece by accident, I nearly throw my phone in disgust. Honestly, I think there's no more wasteful use of time than to read opinions of matrix propaganda. In a perfect world, I would rather everyone receive unbiased information and form their own original thoughts around it. Not to mention, the matrix has many "agents" of misinformation out

The Illusion of Information

there masquerading as journalists, writers, anchors, editors, pundits and so on.

There are many categories and types of information out there, but the two I want to focus on are informational and analytical. Opinion pieces fall under analytical and are thus subject to many unfortunate side effects. Informational is supposed to generally be quite black and white without much area for interpretation. An example of informational news could be your buddy telling you about Wednesday's special dish at a local restaurant this week. It's just information on that particular restaurant, for that particular day. It doesn't necessarily have to involve emotions or any extra analytical interpretation. It may involve emotions, however, if the special happens to be your favorite dish of "honey carrot casserole." Then that information might make you excited for Wednesday. There is a downside however to informational news when it is used to deceive blatantly or inadvertently, and this is where it gets harder to detect, until it's too late. Using the previous example, let's say your friend was mistaken and the Wednesday special you were told about was actually for Tuesday. Now, you look like Booboo the fool and of course, you didn't visit the restaurant on Tuesday because you specifically thought it was for Wednesday. Now you're in the restaurant pouting. All that delicious honey carrot casserole was sold the previous day. How could you have avoided this scenario as tragic as it is? Was the culprit the restaurant or the source of the information? One could argue, you could have easily called the restaurant to verify or done a plethora of other things to make sure you would be in attendance on the right day for that delicious honey carrot casserole. The problem was you took your buddy's information as fact. You trusted him and got burned. The moral of the story here is even with a bit of informational based news, there is a level of responsibility you obtain in your possession. Now, I get this example is a little extreme and I didn't mean to stress you out so much but imagine a few weeks later you find out your

The Illusion of Information

buddy, who knows how much you love honey carrot casserole, lied to you and wanted to buy it all for himself instead. He deliberately told you it was on Wednesday so he could go in the previous day and clean up. Are you ever going to trust him again? Probably not. At least when it comes to restaurant specials anyway. This is how a lot of people are waking up to the lies of the media. It's the catching of the lies way after the fact that is causing a mass awakening. This has happened to me personally a handful of times before my skepticism matured into full blown disgust and distrust.

At any given time on the planet, someone is receiving weaponized information. That is information disguised as beneficial or, in the very least, informative, when it is anything but. Sales pitches, marketing flyers, news broadcasts, your own dentist's advice; information comes at us so fast every day and a lot of it is intentionally false. Sometimes it's known to be false by the sender, most times it's not. I'm saying all this to say become very skeptical of information sources. I would go as far as to say, do not trust your information sources until you have vetted them yourself to some degree. And even after vetting them keep testing them over time. Don't ever become complacent with your news sources. We all fell into this trap of blind trust with our news media because we collectively grew comfortable and way too trusting. Most people are simply not aware of how to break away from the mind leash of believing the talking heads on our televisions. When a news anchor is on your screen and tells you how to think and what to feel, you are being sold something. It could be an ideal, a narrative, or a complete fabrication. The television has been the matrix's greatest selling tool for decades.

Analytical news is an entirely different beast. Most of our mainstream media these days fall under analytical. This is because our mainstream media does much more than provide informational news. They have pundits, experts, journalists and influencers who analyze current events and tell

The Illusion of Information

people what it means. Daytime talk shows and late-night comics gather, process, analyze and then deliver the reference of the world that the matrix would like us to see and believe in; spoon fed like a baby. And we eat it up because it saves us from thinking for ourselves. Comedy is also a great tool for "informing" the public on how we're supposed to feel about any particular subject. For one, it's extremely disarming, and two, sarcasm followed by a laugh track usually cons the mind into installing whatever set of ideas is being presented. It's very intentional and extremely successful.

When I began my awakening from the media, I noticed in real time people regurgitate word for word headlines from the media and spit them out as irrefutable truth, even obvious opinions from celebrity anchors and journalists. A tip on how to interpret analytical news as it comes your way is to examine whether or not what's being presented to you is already in your current belief system. If it is, and biases are being confirmed, you are less likely to put up guards or question it. This is why the grooming of our minds starts at such a young age because their intention is to infiltrate us before we learn the ability to critical think for ourselves.

In the land of confusion, the one true way to become unconfused is to start your path of unlearning. It's a very humbling experience. You have to become ok with knowing that the knowledge you acquired for the majority of your life is most likely incorrect. Even some of your personal life experiences may have been skewed by what you "think" you knew at the time. People hate to hear it but a lot of your experiences as a human on Earth have been directly correlated with how you perceive the world and the people in it. I wrote this section because I wanted you to try to understand that there is other new information to acquire that may go against most of your current beliefs, and it's not that you have to necessarily take on this new information or beliefs and adopt them out of hand. That's not the goal here. The ultimate goal is to expand and broaden the different sources so you can still form your own opinions instead of being spoon fed matrix approved narratives. Not all the matrix approved information is wrong, but an astounding majority is, and not all the alternative media information is right either, I would argue there's a lot of misinformation and propaganda there as well. If you want to truly be independent and minimize your chances of being deceived for a matrix agenda, then you really ought to educate yourself on various perspectives. And in order to open yourself up to do this you have to be willing to understand that you will be unlearning beliefs and paradigms that you've held very strongly for most of your life.

The Illusion of Race

The Illusion of Race

Now it's really time to take the gloves off and piss some people off. As a member of Earth and the human race, I am appalled that in 2025, race issues are what they are, but I get it. This seems to be something isolated more so in the United States than anywhere else. And as disgusted as I am, this is not surprising. The matrix has a stronghold over the people when it comes to the topic of race, and it is sickening to see how much and how far people still easily fall for this. The race traps set by the media, social media, and elsewhere are so obvious to me right now, I do not understand how most of us have not seen and called it out for what it is. This must be addressed because our race "issues" as we know them keep a lot of us vibrationally low and this affects all of us on a collective consciousness level. This book is about awakening. If you are an individual that lives in a state of misunderstanding or judgement of other people, simply due to the color of their skin or ethnicity you are placing yourself in a low vibrational state and sabotaging yourself and others around you tremendously. This goes for anybody and *ALL* races. There is no exclusion of people that have a justification to be racist towards any other group. We need to break away from these matrix traps set for us if we truly wish to become free! Adhering to prejudices and bias towards any single group of people is nothing more than an illusive illusion perpetrated by the matrix. Our physicality is an illusion here. We are all divinely and energetically connected. Hopefully in the next few sections I can debunk and help dismantle any racial disparities and biases you may or may not currently hold. And of course, you can choose to reject anything in this chapter, heck, you may choose to reject anything in this book for that matter, but I hope if you do possess any ill will or disdain for any demographic of people for any reason, I truly hope I can help you overcome such a low and self-damaging state of being.

The Identity Wars

I absolutely *hate* race, but there's nothing more beautiful than the sheer diversity of humans that live here on Earth. I hate race because of the weaponization behind it and how it has been used to divide all of us. So much emphasis and division placed upon what should be our most wonderous traits. The matrix has truly poisoned us with this idea that race should be a prioritizing identifier of who we are and how we should view and separate ourselves. I am of Puerto Rican heritage. Genetically, Puerto Ricans are mainly composed of three major tribes of the world: the Taino (indigenous to Puerto Rico),

Africans and Spanish. I love being Puerto Rican, I love the culture, I love the food, I love the music, and I genuinely appreciate all the good that comes with it. I realize I am in the minority with my thinking, but personally, I place a very small portion of my self-identity upon the race and genetic heritage of the body I was born into. I rarely think about it. My race rarely affects my daily decisions. It's not generally a topic of conversation everywhere I go, and I'm not focused on the racial identity of the people I interact with all the time. I get slightly annoyed when others bring up race because it is virtually always brought up in a negative tone towards others. This is what race has come down to in our conversations; something negative, disparaging and dividing.

Every group of people throughout the world and history has been oppressed and have oppressed others. Don't be naïve enough to believe the genetic group of people that you might belong to (in this life) are free from having committed atrocities in our historical past. No singular group of people are guilt free. And this is ok! The truth is unfortunate, but history is littered with injustice, slavery, murder, and genocide. Mankind's past atrocities can never and will never change. They are forever etched in our history. The question I pose to you is what can we do about it today? The matrix has convinced many people to allow historical events to dictate their current reality and affect their relationships with others. People that have never truly experienced oppression by *historical* standards, yet they live, move and identify as if they are. This is not without support of course from the matrix. The matrix's job here is to take the absolute worst of us, however far or near to the present it is and keep us constantly reminded of it. Think of it as that toxic and abusive ex-partner that we know is bad for us, but we just keep going back. Understanding and being aware of history is one thing, allowing it to dictate your present is a whole other level of an illusive illusion.

Our cultural differences are nothing to get so hysterical about that we can't get along on Earth.

An Elusive Perspective

Unfortunately, culture plays a huge role in the divisiveness across mankind, but it shouldn't. It is the matrix that fans the flames of hate and division among different cultures because it benefits the matrix to do so. I grew up in New York, the melting pot of every culture in the world. I guess I am lucky in that sense to have come up around people of all races, cultures, and backgrounds. Growing up in the Bronx and attending public schools, I had friends of all backgrounds to include Black, Hispanic, Jewish, Muslim and others. Something I did notice however as I got older was how people started to separate themselves as they aged into the higher grades. While we're younger, race and culture don't seem to have any impact on who we make friends with. If you have young children, you may have experienced this phenomenon through them and be reminded of when you were younger. Children really do not take into consideration the color of the skin of other children they meet and choose to play with. As we get older, more of us splinter off into groups of our "own." This is because we start to become influenced by our parents, older relatives and others' patterns and perceptions of the world. Of course, the matrix is right there guiding us into those patterns as well. An argument can be made that tribalism is a natural occurrence because like attracts like, and I would tend to agree to an extent. But I don't think that can explain away the phenomenon we experience with our own children.

When we speak of the Europeans landing in the Americas and the travesties that soon followed, we are not speaking of children that sailed across the Atlantic Ocean to meet a society of other native children. We are speaking of two mature and very different societies clashing during a time of exploration and barbaric conquest. The Europeans had their agenda, and it was very different from the Natives. American history is littered with hateful acts of violence and atrocities. Everyone knows this. The matrix made sure we were taught this history in public schools and society and media goes out of its way to remind us on the daily. There is no room to excuse or minimize anything that happened in this country's past. It is what it is, and we all know it. That was then.

Today, in America we see children give no thought to racial identity every single day. I honestly think there is a lesson to be learned here for us "adults." I believe the innocence of children and how they interact with each other (before corruption and division is programmed in) is the true nature of how humans can and should be interacting. Racism is taught. Every time. Without question. No one is born on this Earth with hate in their heart for any particular group of people. We are all targeted for installation of certain race programming throughout our childhood and into adulthood. I'll get into mine a little later in this chapter, but we all are victims of this programming.

The Vilification of the Races

When the matrix tells you that a group of people hate you and your *"kind,"* it is a bold-faced lie. You can make people hate others by convincing them how much that "group" hates them first or by dehumanizing them. The culture of colonial America was a cesspool of racism, bigotry and prejudice. The Black people brought here and enslaved lived horrible lives. America has a tainted past, but the matrix also had a hand in that. These matrix systems I speak of are *NOT* just applicable to modern times, oh no. The matrix, as I've been describing it, is much older than that. The details are out of the scope of this book and may be in a later edition of this series but understand, systems of control and oppression were always a default program for society.

When it comes to race, there are two lenses to view the world from - a racial lens, and a non-racial lens. It's very easy to discern who is viewing the world through a racial lens most of the time and who isn't. For starters, anyone who can't help but invoke race in every situation but especially in conflict is most likely viewing the world through a racial lens. If a person's skin color or ethnicity is the very first thing you attribute to any kind of disagreement without any other consideration, you may be adversely biased from a racial lens perspective. I theorize that 9 times out of 10, even in the most egregious of conflicts or miscommunication, race is just not a factor, unless it is made to be. There are so many examples of this within matrix media.

In the winter of 2023, there was a young boy at a Kansas City Chiefs game who had the "audacity" to wear a Native headdress and paint his face half black and half red at an NFL game. He was photographed and smeared instantaneously in the media as a racist little white boy that only wanted to spread hate at an NFL game. Turns out the initial photograph that blew up only showed the black

The Illusion of Race

painted side of his face and the chosen headline alluded to black face while also accusing him of disrespecting Native American culture. It also turns out the boy is half Native American. Of course, before the truth came out there was a media frenzy, and the public ate it up without hesitation. How many unsuspecting and naïve people do you think bought into that initial story, without delay? I'm sure quite many. A better question is how many still think that little boy or his parents were blatantly being racist because they never even got the follow-up to the actual truth? Surprisingly more than you'd think. The matrix has a real talent for deceiving the masses and then keeping that veil pulled over their eyes. Debunked lies can remain "true" to many of us. The above example shows how the matrix perpetuates a constant racial lens viewpoint on the people.

Race is made to be so important and prioritized in our society that if you dare to utter the phrase "I don't see race," you are automatically labeled as a bigot and racist. It is a crime to declare that you are capable of taking no notice of the race of a person. But our children do it all the time. Stop and think how ridiculous this is. This is literally the answer to curing the matrix's illusion of racism and yet the matrix gaslights those who stumble onto this solution as racists themselves! Talk about a mind fuck. The psychology and gaslighting behind this prove how far they are willing to go to deceive us all. Morgan Freeman said it best when he said, "I'm going to stop calling you a White man, and I'm going to ask you to stop calling me a Black man," when he was asked how we can stop racism in a television interview with Mike Wallace a while back. Go look it up, it's really a revolutionary clip. This is the solution. It doesn't require race to be totally ignored, but it does provide the opportunity for race to take a few steps back and allow people to identify as human beings first before anything else. Do you think our children, when they're at that most innocent and precious phase, stop and assess the race of the next child before they play with them? No. In that state of

The Illusion of Race

being they have not had any indoctrination or programming yet about stereotypes or who they should or should not be playing with. All the division and self-isolation happens later in life.

At the time of this writing, the matrix is feverishly working on creating an environment in this country in which racism towards White people is widely accepted, normalized and even promoted. If you disagreed with that sentence or it made you feel a certain type of way to read, then you may already be under such conditioning to think that this is justified. This agenda is so powerful, that even White people themselves are falling prey to it. White people are falling into the sunken place of self-hate and taking on guilt for the atrocities of their ancestors. Contrary to popular belief, this is not a good thing. Guilt is and has always been a low vibrational state. There was another time in history where blatant and open racism was allowed and dare I say, celebrated in this country and it was not that long ago. I shouldn't have to get into the details of Jim Crow, segregated bathrooms and buses and so on. As mentioned earlier, our history can never be changed, we can only learn from it. How is it that as a society, we are again, being coerced and groomed by the matrix to allow open discrimination against a certain group of people? Do you not see a pattern emerging here? We are witnessing open racism (again), and it is being sanctioned by media, institutions and the public at large. The matrix is using the history of slavery as justification for racism towards White people and most of society seems to be embracing it with open arms. Some people believe that unless you are an actual White person you cannot be racist; that only White people can be racist. This is the delusion the matrix has pulled over their eyes so the "prejudice" can be justified, but make no mistake, it is racism. No matter how the matrix tries to make you feel better about it, hate is hate.

If you pay attention to the media and its messaging around the topic of race, it is very focused on pointing out very specific racial narratives. The media is the matrix's bullhorn. People who watch the news believe that White people at large are still massively racist as they were decades or centuries ago. This is a façade. The little boy at the football game is just one example that was clearly debunked, but there are so many ambiguous occurrences that happen within the media. I say within the media because that's where these stories are constructed. I say all this to say; As a society, we have become accustomed to labeling people as racist for less and less over the decades. At one point in time, a racist person could be clearly defined and justifiably identified. Members of the KKK, are racist. Firemen who hosed down groups of unarmed Black people were racist. Policemen who sent dogs to attack Black people were racist. Anyone who participated in a violent lynch mob and did the unthinkable, were racist. These were clear & concise instances of racism and hate in this country. Yes, those are very extreme examples, and racism *absolutely* has the ability to be covert, however today, there is a school of thought attempting to label everyone with white skin as a racist by default, regardless of any lack of previous offenses, malicious activity or evidence. We have people buying into this thinking at alarming rates! We have collectively allowed the matrix to bring race back into our psyche with so much malice that it is now on the path to vilifying an entire group of people on the basis of skin color alone (again). Have we not seen this before? Society turned a blind eye in the past for whatever "justifications" that was conjured up at the time and here we are flipping the switch and allowing ourselves to be tricked into doing it again.

The matrix has many different programs out there all executing at once to make different groups of people hate each other. All these programs have different names. You probably are aware of some of them. Each time a program is installed on one of the unsuspecting members of a group, a seed of darkness and low vibration is activated on the planet. I call it a seed of darkness because it creates a fission and

The Illusion of Race

separation of that individual with other seemingly "different" people. In reality, it's the program executing its hate code. When you are coerced into looking at groups of people as separate from you, or your group, and form a viewpoint of malice or contempt you are executing this matrix hate program. You are acting as a literal agent of the matrix when you exercise prejudice towards another group of people.

With all this being said, is racism real? *Absolutely*. Do not conclude that I am under some delusion that there are no living people that use their influence and power to hurt and oppress others based solely on race. Is racism as prevalent as it has been historically? *Absolutely not*. Even in America, when it seems like things are worse than they've ever been racially, understand the media is enforcing, pushing, and promoting a narrative that isn't true. What can be done about the real racism that occurs today? Defeat it with love and understanding, but from afar. You don't have to give into executing hate programming

An Elusive Perspective

in your life. Simply remind the Universe you are not here to experience racism. As we have talked about with the law of attraction you *CAN* repel racist people, scenarios and occurrences from your life if that's what you choose to do; but you must choose it. Applying *more* racism in hopes of defeating racism is a sure path to the longevity of senseless bigotry. And it may seem like a potential solution, but it is not. It is a low vibrational response enabled by the matrix to keep the cycle going, and trust, keeping this cycle going is priority number one to the system. If you have malicious beliefs about another group of people and you believe within your heart that this group is out to get you, guess what situations you will attract in your life? We've been through this before. The Universe will respond to you accordingly and you *WILL* find yourself in situations you do not want to be in, attracted to you by the state of your *MIND*. Above all, hold people accountable for their actions that they conduct in *THIS* lifetime, not the lifetimes of their past ancestors. Don't let the matrix fool you into punishing someone today for the crimes of their lineage.

To be completely honest, I used to have strong adverse feelings towards White people. My environment and upbringing made sure of it. As I mentioned earlier, I grew up with friends of all backgrounds and races, but as I grew older into my early teens and young adult life, whispers of the matrix began creeping in about my "place" in the world as a poor Puerto Rican from the Bronx. I was taught that White people were the harbingers of wealth and went out of their way to keep other races down. It was enforced in music, movies, TV shows, the news and by people I knew in my personal life. I was also taught that having ill will or feelings towards White people isn't racist because my people didn't come from a level of power or influence strong enough to fight back. Therefore, my "racism" was excused. I am seriously ashamed to admit this, but I realize the importance of the revelation. I do not view the world through this racial lens any longer. The relief and happiness of not judging every situation or event (whether positive or negative) on the race of the people around me has allowed me to grow as a spiritual being tremendously. I am writing this, a product of my own awakening, free from the thoughts and therefore, reality, that there are White people out to get me and oppress me in my life. The power you take for yourself when you release this matrix hate program is truly indescribable. The truth is there are people of all backgrounds and races out to oppress others, but there are also people of all backgrounds and races out to help and uplift others. The reality you choose to focus on is the one you give energy that will manifest for you. Which one are *YOU* choosing?

We Are Not Our Physical Bodies

As a spiritual person, I believe in reincarnation. The idea that we are only these physical manifestations is asinine. If you are not familiar with the concept of reincarnation, let me bring you up to speed. The belief of reincarnation is a phenomenon in which our souls can be born into a human body, live a life, die and then return to Earth to live in another body and experience a different life. This cycle repeats until the soul has learned and experienced all it can before ascending forward into a different realm or existence. There are many different theories as to why or the mechanics behind this theory, to include a very dark version where we are trapped here and forced to relive Earth lives as some part of a scheme to siphon off energy from us. But those theories and that one in particular are way out of the scope of this book. The point I'm making

An Elusive Perspective

is, we are not just physical bodies here, we are light bodies, also known as souls. To come to this realm and find trivial differences such as skin color to be such a problem that we separate ourselves with hate is nothing but a by-product of the matrix's illusions. You may find me repeating this sentiment because number one, it's true, and number two, I must make sure I drill into you that the matrix is what makes you hate others. Period.

There's way too much evidence to support the theory that we each have lived lives before here in the past, present and future. There's also evidence our souls transmute into different bodies to include ethnicities and genders. For instance, there is the famous 9/11 reincarnation story of a boy named Cade. When he was very little and started talking, his parents reported that he used to obsess over airplanes and tall buildings and would say strange things like he fell from a tall building and died. His parents couldn't understand what he was talking about or where he seemed to be getting this information, but after a few years of this obsession and further research, they concluded that he was someone that was killed in the 9/11 attacks. He was even able to produce the name of his past life, and it was verified with the official 9/11 victim list. The boy successfully named someone that died, and the parents swear he was never provided this information.

There's another example of a Caucasian boy named Luke who remembered his past life of being a Black Woman that died in a building fire. Very similar to Cade's story in that he just started to talk about being someone else and knowing things someone of his young age couldn't possibly know. It turned out the woman died in the Paxton hotel fire in Chicago in 1993. Luke talked about how he had to jump off the burning building, he was even able to identify a picture of the woman from a lineup of random women. He even said, "I remember when I took this picture." You can look these and other reincarnation stories up for yourself online. The point

I'm getting at is if you are a White male today, you could've been a Black female in a past or will become one in a future life, or vice versa. This proves race is just a physiological condition of who you are today, but not in the grand scheme of your eternal existence.

There are various spiritual teachings that portray our true form as light bodies or light beings. And this temporary existence we experience in these human bodies is a very small portion of our true being. A "light body" refers to a concept found throughout history, linked with the idea that human beings possess not only a physical body but also a subtle, energy-based body composed of light or higher vibrational frequencies. The concept has its origins in ancient belief systems and has been explored in different forms across cultures and time. In ancient Egyptian religion, the "ka" represented the spiritual double of a person, which exists independently from the physical body. In Hinduism and Buddhism, the notion of the "subtle body" or "energy body" is central to their teachings, comprising the chakras and nadi. Today, the idea of the light body has become entangled with New Age spirituality and is often associated with the pursuit of higher consciousness, enlightenment, and transcendence of physical limitations. It continues to be a subject of exploration and interpretation in modern spiritual practices.

Now tell me, if the concept of light bodies is true, where does race fit in here? Do you think there are different races of light bodies? Perhaps our light bodies are intermingled with the ethnicity of our physical body? Personally, I just can't fathom it. Our physical forms, as we know them, are temporary. I understand I might seem eccentric here, because there are many people who have most of their personal identity tied up with their racial identity, but I don't buy into race this strongly anymore. I do not believe race as the matrix tells us is as important or should hold the weight that it seemingly does in our society and lives. This concept of race in humanity has been perverted and abused over the centuries and used as the primary divisive tool. Honestly, I believe the world would be a much better place if everyone could learn to ignore race and acknowledge culture. Culture transcends race, since many races can belong to the same culture. America is a prime example of this. This is not even asking a lot, but one day the race issue will finally be put to bed, and humans of all the cultures of the world will be able to co-exist without animosity or malice towards each other. I know in my soul this is coming soon.

When you think of us as light bodies, or spiritual beings having a human experience, this concept of race seems so trivial and problematic, as it should be. Many of us have become so lost in our temporary genetic makeup that we spend lifetimes divided over the level of melanin in our skin. When you stop and think about this, and I mean really think about this, you can begin to grasp how low the matrix is willing to go to have us fight and divide ourselves. I say this with 100% conviction; race is an illusion.

The Illusion of Race

We are all light beings experiencing a human life. I challenge you to make the effort to see people as light beings first, then human, then take notice of race if you absolutely must. The judgements passed onto unsuspecting people on the basis of race alone are keeping many of us in a low vibratory state and does not serve us any benefits at all. It doesn't matter if you think you are justified. It doesn't matter if you have life experience with a particular group to feel you are justified. If you hold contempt for any particular race of people for any reason, you are adding to the matrix's race hate programming and you are unbalanced. Start fresh today, break the hate programming and free yourself of the burden of defaulting to someone who passes judgement on others for the simplest things.

LUCID PERSPECTIVES

The Illusion of Race

Manifesting

Manifesting

In case you weren't aware, you are manifesting all the time. We all are. *Everyday*. When you wake up in the morning, you start manifesting. When you're eating lunch in the middle of the day, you're manifesting. When you're sitting on the toilet bowl pinching off a log, you are manifesting. The difference between someone who is living a life they desire and someone who is not can be broken down into one word. Intention. There are two types of manifestation. Intentional manifestation, and Unintentional manifestation.

Which Type of Manifestor Are You?

Most of us here on Earth are Unintentional Manifestors (we'll shorten that to U.M. for simplicity and I.M. respectively). What this means is you have no real direction where you want your life to go, and you are not actively pursuing or executing any plan on how to achieve anything. Most of these people simply live their lives and totally rely on external influences to direct them in any one direction. These people will still have desires, or wants or maybe even dreams, but as a U.M. they have not made the choice to take the reins and steer their own life. External influences for this group can be parents, religious affiliation, the school they attend, the city they live in, their friends and co-workers, the culture they are members of; the list is endless. Understand, U.M.'s can also be rich and live luxurious lives as well. To be a U.M. does not mean you are poor or struggling financially at all. It means you are not aware of the power of your thoughts and mind, and you are executing a program installed from your youth. Think of people born into wealth. Wealth is all they know, so they can live with these luxuries and still be a U.M. The program of wealth is installed into their psyche and so they can manifest other scenarios and problems that are not tied to wealth. Admittedly, most U.M.s do struggle financially because they are running the program they were born into, which for most of the population is a program of lack and scarcity. The U.M. has good days and bad days and lives life like everyone else. They still manifest in their life; it's just the default programming they were dealt with when they arrived on Earth that is the program they are executing unintentionally.

Then we have Intentional Manifestors (I.M.). These people have decided to take the reins of their life and go out and make something shake. They understand that no one will care more about their success and dreams than they will. They understand that it's who they are on the inside that will bring them what they want. They also understand that despite external circumstances, they can overcome. These people may fail many times over their life but never lose faith in their dreams and goals. Keep in mind, this group doesn't necessarily have to live in wealth and luxury either. You can be an I.M. and still struggle with your manifestations; but what makes you different from the U.M. is that you know you are in control and can switch up and change your direction. Although you may not be where you want to be currently, you have the tools and knowledge necessary to get where you want to be. These people do not make excuses or shrug off the responsibilities they have over their life. All failures they experience are of their own creation and they use them as learning experiences.

So how do you make the transition from a U.M. to an I.M? Certainly, reading this book helps. But the key is in the word intentional. Assess yourself

Manifesting

and see if you can identify which of the two types of manifestation groups you fit into. Be honest with yourself. This can be the start of the turning for your life. There is no in between. You are either a U.M. or an I.M. If your self-assessment revealed that you are an Unintentional Manifestor, we got you covered. First, make a choice right here and now while you're reading this that you will be an Intentional Manifestor from here on out. Make this declaration. You can say it to yourself, or you can say it out loud. Whichever works for you. It's not enough to just say it, however, you must be *IT*. Believe in your statement. No half-assing or doubts. Starting today, you will have full intention of manifesting the trajectory of your life from here on until you leave this Earth. How do you know if you even done this part correctly? If you feel empowered, you did it right. If you don't feel empowered with the declaration that means apart of you doesn't believe and you have to dig inside and reveal what it is about

An Elusive Perspective

you that is stopping you from believing you are absolutely in control.

Admittedly, I was a U.M. until about my mid-twenties. Up to that point, I was on autopilot. Of course, I had desires and wants. There were things I liked and didn't like. But life as a U.M. meant I was very much influenced by everything and everyone around me. U.M.s are true products of their environment. As a U.M., I was also under the impression that the world in general was out to get me, my kind, and keep me poor while denying me every luxury I ever wanted. I was under the belief system that there was someone out there that had the power to keep from me all that I wanted. This belief unfortunately discourages most U.M.s from even trying most of the time. Because if you believe someone else has the power to deny you, why should you even try? As a U.M., things happened *TO* me. Events happened *TO* me. People did bad things *TO* me. I was denied credit because I didn't make enough money. I didn't have enough money because my job paid me low wages. I was paid low wages because I had no real value to them. I had no real value to them because I had no real value for myself. I had no real value for myself because I was born into an environment that didn't resonate with high vibrations. Of course, writing this now I can feel the ridiculousness of these words because I am in a much higher state today. As a matter of fact, we *ALL* are. All of us are capable of the highest states of vibration, you just have to be aware of it and have intention for it!

For many of you who are probably reading about this concept for the first time, this book may very well be your first introduction to an I.M. lifestyle. Mine was reading the book and seeing the film "*The Secret*" by Rhonda Byrne. This time in my life of my mid-twenties was literally the first time I ever heard the concept of "thoughts creating things" and the power of your mind reflecting in your subjective reality. I was deeply intrigued by the notion that I can be in control of everything in my life and that all this time I just didn't know it. It resonated with me tremendously. It made so much sense. Although I was living as a U.M., something in me felt wrong about how the world worked and how I believed things to be. Somehow, I always knew there was a real solution to getting what you want and making positive things happen. I honestly believe it was this lingering idea that a solution did exist that made "The Secret" manifest in my life. Even as a U.M., I didn't live my life as a hopeless person. I believed in good things, and good people. I also like to think I have a good sense of morality, so perhaps it was this "gratitude" in me that helped manifest the book. I didn't immediately begin implementing all that The Secret had to teach. Actually, it was a few more years before I really started practicing what was in it. But it planted the seed that would eventually help me grow into the person that I am today; The person writing this book and passing on this information to others. If you haven't heard of The Secret, I plead you to look into it. I will include a list of books and material at the end of this book as a reference that I really think you should investigate further. But we've dodged the point long enough. Ok, so you made the declaration to be an Intentional Manifestor, so now what? Glad you asked.

Manifestation 101

Now that you have made the first step, let's dive into the world-famous double-slit experiment so we can pile on some real-world science shit onto this new understanding. I'm going to keep this as layman's terms as possible without losing the sciencey-ness of the quantum mechanics of what this experiment told us about this reality, so bear with me. In the 1960's a scientist by the name of Claus Jönsson, conducted what we call the modern version of the double slit experiment. There was a version conducted in the early 1800's that served a different

An Elusive Perspective

purpose. In this experiment, the goal was to determine whether light photons act as a wave or particle. Keeping it simple, waves in this context are energy and particles are matter. The experiment was conducted as follows. Imagine two plates side by side to each other, but one has two open slits. A light was beamed through the plate with the slits to record how the light would look on the other plate. The pattern of light on the whole plate would determine if the light photons were acting as a particle or wave.

DOUBLE SLIT EXPERIMENT

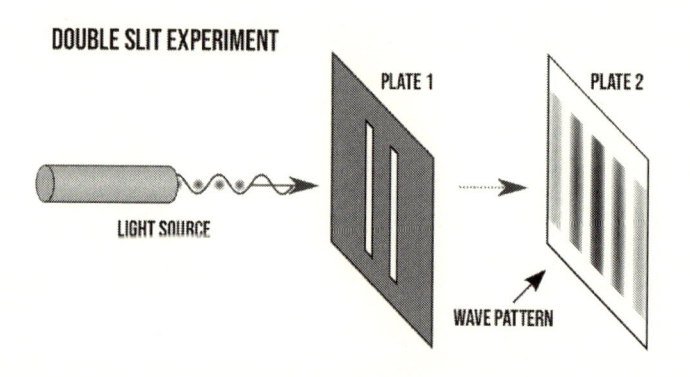

PLATE 1 PLATE 2

LIGHT SOURCE

WAVE PATTERN

Figure 7-1 "No Observation Tools"

Of course, this is all performed with very scientific equipment and machines. I can't imagine anyone can try this with household items because there is a huge requirement on how to conduct the observation of the experiment. The details are way out of the scope of this book, but long story short, when the test is performed without careful measuring or "observation" of the photons as they enter the slits, the pattern on the other side mimics a wave as shown in the first diagram. However, when a careful measuring tool is used or an "observation" is applied to the experiment, the pattern mimics how matter and particles would scatter, known as the particle pattern as shown below.

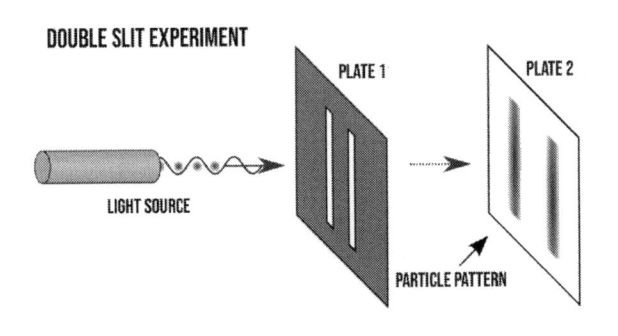

Figure 7- 2 "Observation Tools"

For more information on this experiment and further details on the quantum mechanics of it all, you'll have to do your own research. But what this essentially proves to us is that our observation of this reality *CHANGES* things. Science is about repeating experiments and getting the same results every time if the parameters don't change. However, in this experiment the results change when an attempt is made to observe the photons entering the slits. When there is no observation, the wave patterns emerge. The observation and changing of the results are more casually known as "the collapsing of the wave function."

So, what does this mean for manifestation? Let's break this down. Our thoughts are waves. They radiate away from our craniums and vibrate out to our external world. Like the double split experiment, if you emit your thought waves and then *OBSERVE* them with emotions and intention, you will collapse the waves into particles! *HELLO!* This is what we've been talking about for this entire book! The double slit experiment proved to us that our thoughts are things that we can manifest for real in our subjective realities if we only acknowledge them! That Bugatti we spoke of earlier, it starts out as a thought in your mind and with your emotion and intention you can collapse that wave of thought energy into matter for yourself. This is how science backs up the law of attraction and the law manifestation. This is real applicable science! Make your declaration, become an intentional manifestor and go out there and create your dreams.

Gratitude

Gratitude

Too many people sleep on gratitude, but it is possibly the most powerful emotion you can use in your manifestation arsenal. If you are one of those unfortunate souls on Earth that rarely feel gratitude, for whatever reason, train your mind to start intentionally making it a habit *NOW*. Gratitude is essentially a shortcut to a positive and higher vibrational mindset. In my personal and professional opinion, it's faster to achieve and experience than the other higher vibration emotions. You can feel gratitude every day, for any reason and it will help and work in your favor to manifest your dreams and desires. There are a couple reasons why maintaining a true state of gratitude is a shortcut to literally achieving almost anything. First, it keeps you in a higher state of frequency and vibration. As discussed previously, this is the one and true way to manifest anything you want. And secondly, it reminds you of your very real present. You are required to be aware of your present to gauge and prepare for your future. So many of us get lost in either the past or future and completely ignore our current state! Most of us dwell on traumas and negative experiences from our past or focus on anxieties and fears about our future. Meanwhile, ignoring your present makes you completely powerless to manifest anything different than your traumatic past or fearful future. Gratitude forces you to focus on the now, and when you focus on the now, you're more attuned to realizing all that you have to be grateful for.

Here is how you can practice gratitude every day. Stop and think about your blessings right this minute. Don't over-complicate it, and don't take this opportunity to think about things you do not have or what you feel you are lacking in life; this is not the time for that. Count your blessings right now. It could be as simple as a roof over your head. Food in the fridge. Clothes on your back. Health! Your ability to walk. Your ability to speak, hear, or see. All these things you can feel gratitude for right NOW. Of course, there are people (and you may be one of them) who are lacking some of the things I just listed, and that's OK! Find the things YOU can be grateful for in your life at this very moment. This can be a very specific and tailored exercise to your current situation. Even if you feel you have nothing to be grateful for in your current circumstance, I promise you, you absolutely do. Unfortunately, I can't peer into your life and pinpoint whatever that is out. You must be able to discern and execute this for yourself. Once you do it, hold on to that feeling of gratitude and practice feeling that emotion every day for as long as you can. Even if it's just a few minutes a day to start. It will get easier, and it will become second nature. This exercise is designed to regularly lift you out of any low or negative vibrations and lift you up into those higher manifesting frequencies.

An Elusive Perspective

Don't become confused. Having gratitude for your present doesn't mean you cannot attract a better future; and it most certainly is not meant to spark any type of envy of others who may have or be what you want. In fact, expressing and having gratitude for your present is literally how you attract future goals or desires to your present. As discussed earlier, you can FEEL gratitude for your future goals and desires right now. By aligning with the frequency of gratitude for your future self today, you hack the system and manifest it quickly. This is why you should begin practicing feeling gratitude for where you currently are, so the transition to feeling gratitude for the things you have yet to achieve will be smoother. As we discussed prior, you must be active in the vibration of the lifestyle you want to attract. Some like to call this "fake it till you make it." I disagree with the statement because it implies deceit and if you don't believe it, it won't manifest. Think of it this way; you are not faking it; you are being it. I understand this may be difficult for some to grasp but over time I'm confident it will make much more sense to you.

I personally make gratitude a part of my daily experience and you can too. I would argue it's probably better to practice a state of gratitude if things are constantly going "wrong" in your life than if they aren't. For instance, say you're on a long road trip and you get a flat tire. Immediately you'll begin cursing out the car, the road, the squirrels etc. But then you remember, you have a spare in the back and not only that, you know how to change it. You think to yourself how really screwed you'd be if you didn't have that spare and immediately your emotional state changes to gratitude for the spare. Some call this looking on the brighter side and it is a remarkable strategy to lifting your vibration because it works. Remember, you are not trying to manifest the worse scenario, you are simply acknowledging that you are grateful for your present circumstance. You may be surprised how the Universe will respond in tandem with your emotional state at a time of "misfortune."

An Elusive Perspective

Using that same example, let's say you don't have the spare. Now what? You can still focus and find a positive. Be glad it's daylight outside and not pitch black, or that it's not raining, or that it's not too cold or hot outside. There is always a positive spin that can be applied to unfortunate moments. I understand this might take some time to get used to, but it is very effective once perfected and applied daily. Once this tactic becomes second nature to you, you'll find that your day to day will be filled with less and less unfortunate events. Don't get me wrong they will still come, however your mindset in dealing with them when they do can quickly turn those negatives into positives and the Universe will respond accordingly. This is natural law; it has no choice but to react to you. Don't forget that.

Be Grateful Now, So You Can Be Grateful Later

Several years ago, I worked at The Pentagon. When I got the message that I was hired I was ecstatic and filled with gratitude. What's bizarre is I remember fantasizing about working in The Pentagon for years prior to that moment because one, it's cool (at least I considered it to be) and two, I'm a huge movie buff and love military, government, and spy movies. Almost every military or spy movie had that B-roll overhead drone shot of The Pentagon and whenever I saw it, I just felt a connection to it for whatever reason. I would talk with my girlfriend (at the time) about working in important military buildings frequently since that's what I did back then and somehow The Pentagon would always creep into the conversation. I even remember being very confident for some reason that I could very well end

An Elusive Perspective

up working there. The point I'm making is I felt a sense of pride and gratitude for the role I had before actually landing The Pentagon position, and this gratitude eventually led to the opportunity and reality of me actually working there. Fast forward to my time there and I remember walking the halls of this huge important building and sometimes I would just be in awe of everything. The magnitude of the halls and size of the building itself is insane. I would take self-guided tours around the building and just take in the museum-like atmosphere and be so high on gratitude and vibrations of appreciation for where I was at that time of my life. It really was invigorating and hard to describe in words. I guess if you can imagine yourself in a place, city or town that you've always wanted to visit or be a part of and then you're there. Try to think of the excitement and gratitude you would have. That's what I experienced every day for about three years. And I really attribute that to my attitude and what I was manifesting for years before that.

Solutions Will Reign Down Upon You

Another benefit to being grateful as much as you possibly can is over time you will become much better at finding solutions for your problems when they arise. Solutions to almost any issue will just download right into your brain because you flipped that low vibration switch of complaining and feeling down into thinking on the brighter side. Because of this, solutions will show themselves feverishly. Sometimes I surprise myself when a problem manifests in my life and almost instantly I have a way forward for a resolution. Think of a time where everything was going wrong in your life, mishap after mishap after mishap. We've all had those type of periods in our life. Where problems just seem to keep accumulating on top of each other with no solution in sight. Now if you can remember, think back to those times. Were you being grateful every day? Were you actively looking for the positives? Probably not. Being grateful helps your mind attract solutions. Being ungrateful does the opposite, it pushes solutions away from you and invites more problems and scenarios where you can just be more ungrateful.

I lost count of how many times a "problem" would arise in my life and a solution would immediately manifest. Unforeseen bills can pop up out of nowhere and somehow a check in the mail or a client would drop in my lap that could cover it. Believe it or not, sometimes the problems would even disappear. Seriously. Once I received a city tax bill in the mail, I put it aside and forgot about it. Somehow, I stumbled upon it across my desk and it was a few weeks late with a penalty. I logged into the website to pay it, and it just wasn't in the system. I wasn't going to ask any questions either. Perhaps it was an error on the city, I can't call it, all I know is I couldn't pay the bill online and it wasn't being pulled up with the bill number and it wasn't in my account as a pending bill. The website said I didn't owe anything. Who am I to argue with that? Most of us have absolutely no problem manifesting issues or problems in our lives and don't question it when they pop up, but when something good happens we have all the questions and skepticism. Once you become a person filled with gratitude for any situation, you'll start to see magical moments like these in your life. And what's better is not questioning it or feeling undeserving of the positive event but accepting it as easily as when problems arise.

Try to understand the power behind gratitude. There was this other time in my life, where I made a huge purchase with a department credit card. I was enticed with a 0% interest for two or maybe three years' time frame on this purchase. I was ecstatic, I really needed the appliances and on top of that, I figured three years is more than enough time to pay it off without making a single interest payment. Cut to three years later and of course, I had totally forgotten about that purchase and the impending deferred interest that was about to be smacked onto my credit card balance. On this particular day that I logged in to make a payment, I was immediately flabbergasted to see an extra $3,000.00 dollars of balance there that wasn't the last time I checked. This had to be a mistake at best or fraud at worst because there was no way this could happen. After some quick investigating, I realized it was that deferred interest for that large charge I made three years earlier. Three. Whole. Thousand. Dollars. For a brief moment, I felt like I was having a panic attack. This didn't make any sense. I figured I could call the vendor and bitch them out or try to make some case as to why this was unfair. My mind was literally trying to find a way out of this predicament. I honestly felt like this was the worst thing that ever happened to me in my life (it obviously wasn't). After I calmed myself down and realized this was the bed I made and had to lay in, I realized I needed to find a way to justify this event and improve my life over it. I needed to find something in this event to be grateful for. I needed to spin this into a positive and I needed to do it fast or else it could've ruined my entire week or month. I took that moment to learn to never, ever allow deferred interest purchases to go past the deadline. Apparently, I needed this to happen to me and for me to actively look for a positive spin on it, in order to feel gratitude for the event. And not only was I better for it, in addition to paying attention to all zero interest purchases (or simply avoiding them when I can), I was able to pay off those appliances and that $3,000.00 deferred interest not long after that. I understand this may seem like a rough route to take when something so unfortunate can happen to you, but understand, it is in these moments and how you deal with them that allow you to become the best version of yourself. For me, personally, I could not spin that event any other way but to take it on the chin and learn from the mistake. My acceptance of it (after my initial denial of course) and gratefulness allowed me to learn a valuable lesson in finance purchases and overcome the burden eventually altogether. Try and think of a time when something bad or very unfortunate happened to you. What did you do about the situation? Did you allow it to destroy you? Did you learn from it at all?

Gratitude provides a huge benefit to being healthy overall. Being grateful puts your mind and spirit on the higher vibrations and frequencies. The body has no choice but to be relaxed and stress free when your mind is vibrating higher. In case the point hasn't hit for you yet, we are trying to keep ourselves in a high vibration for most of our day and lives. This is the true way to achieving everything that you desire. Remember, you want to shift into being an intentional manifestor. Be grateful and practice gratitude daily, watch the positive impacts it brings into your life. In my personal opinion, I feel like gratitude should be one of the top three life hacks of all time. It really is a shortcut to happiness.

Gratitude

Fear of Failure

Failure is your friend. Unfortunately, most of us treat it as a foe. Collectively we all need to dismantle and break this programming. Fear of failure serves no purpose. The reason this chapter is in this book of awakening is because we as a collectively need to understand that trying is a necessity of life. Toddlers who are learning to walk do not have a fear of falling. If you've ever watched a toddler continue to try walking after falling you would understand this. That fear of falling isn't even a factor. We need to re-adopt this mindset within ourselves in our adult lives. We need to look at the tasks and goals before us and push forward despite the possibility of failure and push forward in the face of failure.

An Elusive Perspective

When I was in basic training in the Navy, I didn't find any of the courses, classes or training all that difficult. Honestly, I felt like it was too easy. Except for one mandatory portion. The swimming qualifications. Yes, I joined the Navy not knowing how to swim. At the time I figured if I was ever going to learn, the Navy would be the place. I joined basic training in fall of 2005. I believe basic was 8 or 9 weeks back then and my graduating class of sailors was scheduled to wrap up right before Christmas that year. After graduation we were slated to have leave for a few weeks into the new year, go home to see our families and then back out to the fleet to officially start our Navy careers. The details are fuzzy, but my division went for our swimming quals somewhere in early to mid-November. I could not pass the swim quals to save my life (literally). I obviously failed on swim day. Most of everyone else passed so they went on to the other parts of basic training. Because I was among a handful of helpless swimmers, I had to continue to go and try to pass the swim quals every other day (schedule permitting) until I could pass. This went on for a few weeks before I was known as the one guy that could not swim in my entire division. As the weeks went on and I still could not get qualified, my RDC's (Recruit Division Commander) started to advise me that if I didn't get these swim quals in time, I wouldn't be allowed to graduate on time, not get my leave, be held back over the holidays in the barracks over into the new year and have to start basic training all over again with a whole new class and a new division. This was unacceptable.

Something switched. I was losing time. I was also losing attempts to try because while I was still trying to get the quals, I had other scheduled training to still complete with everyone else. I remember when I was down to my last three attempts. It was during the last week before graduation. After this week, the pool building was going to close for a few weeks over the holiday. By this point I was able to get the 50-yard swim qualification. It was treading water for 5 minutes that I was literally almost

An Elusive Perspective

drowning in every time, and yes, I had plenty of experience with burning lungs due to lack of oxygen (not fun at all). The goal was simple on paper. Get in the water, tread water for 5 whole minutes and require no help from the Navy divers who were supervising. If they had to save your life because you were drowning, you failed. Oh, and you get one chance per attempt, no do-overs for that day. Staying in Great Lakes, Illinois over Christmas and New Year's in the Navy barracks was not going to be my life, let alone doing bootcamp all over again. I spent up the last two of three attempts and I was down to the wire now. I believe it was a Thursday. My last attempt to tread water for 5 minutes or else I'd get left behind, not go home and be freezing my ass off in Naval Station Great Lakes for a few weeks before I start basic all over again.

I remember it like it was yesterday. Failure was not an option. On the morning of my last available attempt, the rest of the division was restless because the excitement of finishing bootcamp and graduating was literally days away. The last obstacle for the whole division was the Navy's final test called *Battle Stations,* and I still have not wrapped up my water treading. Thinking back on this now and reliving these moments is surreal because a part of me honestly felt like there was no chance I was going to fail despite my immaculate record of failures. I knew what it felt like to fail so many times, for some reason I was dead set on succeeding.

I jumped in the water, determined to tread it for 5 minutes no matter what. I didn't care how hot my lungs got, how tired my arms were, how exhausted my legs were. I was going to tread that water for 5 minutes, show these divers that I can pass and earn my leave and go home for the holidays. And I did just that. The diver congratulated me and told me of all the treading water tests he administered that mine was the most trifling and sloppiest he'd ever seen in his entire career. He said I looked like I was drowning the entire time but since I stayed afloat, he had no choice but to pass me. I was ecstatic and I didn't care about any of that, all I was hyped about was that I passed, and I was going to graduate on time!

I ran back to the barracks excited to share the news with the rest of my division. I forgot to mention one of my closest friends in basic, Seaman Recruit (SR) Miller. We were very close, and he was ridiculously invested in my swimming quals throughout the course of basic training. He was the black sheep of the division, always getting into trouble, always being the rebel, always in controversy and pissing off the RDC's the most. I was the total opposite, always trying to be a ghost, stay hidden, not make a scene, do what I was told and get the hell out of basic. I'm not sure how we clicked but we did. When I got back to the barracks, he saw my face and instantly knew I passed. He was so excited for me he lifted me up off the ground and yelled to the rest of the division "Hey everyone! Orozco passed his swim quals!" The whole division stopped in their tracks and looked directly at us. Most gave a lazy grunt as if they didn't care, others surrendered a barely audible celebration, and I think one or two people clapped once for me. Overall, his announcement fell on deaf ears, and it was not very well received, but I think of what SR Miller did for me that day from time to time and I hope wherever he is, he is living his best life, is achieving all his goals and is happy. We never stayed in touch after basic. Thank you, SR Miller of Division 029, Graduating Navy basic training class of December 2005, Great Lakes, Michigan.

I shared this story because it reminded me of the toddler learning to walk. I kept failing the swim test, but I didn't care, and I knew to be successful I had to keep trying no matter what. The matrix has this gift of instilling this fear in us as we mature in age that paralyzes us of achieving our best selves. It could be due to our environment, our peers, the media; there's a plethora of reasons why as we age, we begin to develop these fears which stop us in our tracks. I would argue that it's not necessarily a bad thing to have that fear of failure, but it is bad to allow it to stifle your progress in life and not even try. In your awakening journey, it's important to understand fear of failure is normal, but it should not be a deterrent. Most importantly don't worry about what others think! If you're a strong or at least decent swimmer you probably read my story and thought of how ridiculous it was that I was basically a grown man that couldn't tread water. Maybe you learned to swim at a very young age, and it was never an issue in your entire life. We are all different and have different abilities and clutches. Our unique qualities and fears are what make us diverse and stronger. You may have a particular fear that no one else has. So what? If you overcome that, it is an accomplishment for YOU and no one else. My entire division had basically passed their swim quals the second week of training (to include SR Miller) while I struggled the entire 9 weeks. To them it wasn't that big of a deal, but to me, it was the difference between success and another 9 weeks of being held back. Your struggles

Fear of Failure

are your struggles and unfortunately most people are not going to provide you with the courtesy or means to overcome them. That is generally a feat we must overcome for ourselves. The fear of what others think of us is arguably the most common type of fear that we as a collective allow to hinder us. It's time for that to stop. Make a declaration now that you will not allow fear of failure or fear of what others think to hinder your gifts to thrive. Tell the Universe that you are ready to push forward and become your best self by not allowing fear to get in the way.

Also, something to keep in mind is that the emotion of fear is a very low vibration. It is down there with the worst of the worst emotions. Fear is a stagnating energy. No wonder the matrix goes out of its way to make sure the populace en masse is experiencing some type of fear one way or another. It serves them to keep us in a fear state where we aren't in the best state of mind to thrive, achieve and ascend into our best selves. It is an act of rebellion towards the system today to be free of fear and pursue

An Elusive Perspective

your goals and dreams. Lastly, don't be impeded by your failures. Keep failing. Every time you fail, you have learned what not to do to achieve your goals and you are only getting closer to success. I know it sounds very cliché, and you've heard it many times before, but it is true. The more you fail, the more you know how to succeed.

Stop and think about whatever it is right now that you've been scared to do. It could be following a dream, starting a business, reaching out to someone, going to the gym. I know there is a fear in you right now, something you wish you could overcome and conquer for the sake of your own happiness, but you've been allowing your fear to hold you back. Take this time right now and make a declaration to yourself that you will no longer allow this irrational fear to hold you back. It's been long enough. You've lost time. You're on your last attempt like I was before passing my swim quals and going home for the holidays. And if you try and fail, so what?! Get up and do it again!

Fear of Failure

10

Logic vs Emotion

Logic vs Emotion

Ah yes, the Yin and Yang of the bane of all human existence. The brittle dance between logic and emotion paints a symphony of enigma via the dualistic nature of the complexities of paradox. Logic and emotions were both meant for each other and destined to be mortal enemies. I believe it's this paradox that should help us understand the situation we put ourselves in when we came here. Logic and emotion are comparable to our minds and hearts, respectively. We interpret our reality with our minds (logic), and we feel our reality with our hearts (emotion). This is why as humans we struggle with decisions split between the two. We constantly face this paradoxical conflict within us daily. You know the saying, "The heart wants what the mind can't have." We've all made emotionally driven choices that we came to regret later, and we've all denied ourselves in the pursuit of discipline and making wiser choices. One of the desperate goals of the matrix is to program you to emphasize one over the other. It is with this imbalance of either too logical or too emotional thinking that persuades us to live in disharmony. This is yet another way to divide the masses and impair our ability to effectively communicate and understand each other when we find ourselves at odds. If someone is working out of logic most of the time, emotions like empathy take a backseat, making this person cold, difficult, calculated, and seemingly heartless. Obviously not a person who is operating within harmony around others. If someone is working out of emotion most of the time, they are unable to consider other viewpoints, potential solutions to their problems, and lack the ability to entertain or receive alternative information which may be beneficial to them. Being overly emotional does not offer harmony around others either. An overly emotional person is prone to manipulation, coercion and self-destruction.

I would argue that most conflicts between people are fought on opposite ends of this dualistic Spectrum. Take married couples for example, how many times have you been in a disagreement with your partner and no matter who is saying what it seems like neither person is listening? It doesn't work. Most arguments in marriages are a perfect example of when both partners are operating on opposite ends of the two extremes. The balance is off. This is far from a self-help book for marriages, but the key is to find balance and common ground here. In a marriage, it's safe to say that generally the male is the logical partner, and the female is the emotional partner. This is a "general" fact. I emphasize general because of course there are exceptions and instances where these roles are reversed. In a union such as a marriage, there is naturally going to be some sort of dualistic arrangement and lo and behold a logical male and an emotional female seem to be the

An Elusive Perspective

consensus the Universe decided upon. But what does this mean? It means even within what seems to be disharmony to the untrained eye, the Universe is perfect and in balance despite our perceptions!

Wait, didn't you just say when a couple is arguing that they are off balance? Yes, I did but remember everything exists in fractals. On a personal level, we all have moments of imbalance when we internalize conflict between logic and emotion and lean towards one. In our marriages we do the same. Instead of it being just ourselves for instance, it's now scaled to two people. The next dimension "up" if you will. What I'm getting at is even in our instances of imbalance, whether personal or in a partnership or otherwise, on a greater scale, everything is still as perfect as it should be. The Yin and Yang of duality is omnipresent. Now, if you go back and start reading this chapter from the top again, you will notice that I started off on how leaning towards one side creates an imbalance and now I'm saying even with imbalance the Universe is still

Logic vs Emotion

balanced and that is the fucking paradox shit I've been talking about (pardon my French). This shit makes no sense and yet it does!

Let's come down a few notches because we can easily get lost in space if we stay there. Given the same set of facts, two logical people will generally agree on an issue when pure and sound logic is at play. Likewise, given the same set of facts, two emotional people will generally agree on an issue when pure and sound emotion is at play. Most of the time, however, we do not get the same set of facts! This is by matrix design. This is why our political system is so far gone. We have a melting pot of different sets of facts, being processed by either too emotional or too logical people and everyone is having conversations about the same things which they see differently. There is a better way, but first we need to understand why logic and emotion are imperative to construct our reality and why each should be recognized and applied properly with intention.

An Elusive Perspective

Pros & Cons of Logic

Logic gives us the black and white, pure reasoning, cold calculations and colors within the lines of rationality. A logical person has the ability to determine the likely consequences of their actions and weighs the risks of those decisions. Logical people have an aversion to being exploited by appeals to emotions such as fear, greed or empathy, which is why they can seem heartless at times. It works to their benefit when defending against narcissistic manipulation. Critical thinkers are also able to process information in a way that minimizes deceit. Not saying that critical thinkers can't be fooled, because they most definitely can, it just makes it harder when dealing with a logical leaning mindset.

The flaw with logic is when it comes to manifestation, it has little to no imagination. Logic takes what is and has very little ability to infer alternative scenarios. Logic will have you looking at your surrounding environment and believe that is all there is to see, because that is all you've ever seen. A logical mind focuses way too much on the past and present and has a hard time forecasting opposing futures. If most of my life I have experienced poverty and struggle, then logic dictates that tomorrow and the day after will be the same. My variables are set, the equation is written, and there is no wiggle room. As you can see this does not allow much growth or enthusiasm for the near or long-term future. Although this is a flaw for manifesting, it is critical for being in the present and acknowledging what is in the now. We talked about this with gratitude. You can use logic to help you identify what in your current life you can be grateful for. Use logic to understand the positives in your life right now and use the power of gratitude to manifest more situations to be grateful for.

Pros & Cons of Emotion

Highly emotional people have much empathy for those around them and are generally caring and nurturing. Emotional people are highly prone to manipulation because they are open to the lower vibrational frequencies such as guilt trips and shame. Certainly, emotions have no quarrel with tossing all logic out the window and festering solely on itself. We have all seen and experienced this. Are you happy right in this moment? If the answer is yes, you are vibrating optimally, and you are attracting opportunities for higher vibrational energy.

Unlike logic, emotions are FULL of imagination. How many of us conjured up imaginary situations that were the furthest from the actual objective truth? I know I have. Emotions can be dangerous, because they can be very powerful when resonating at the lower frequencies. Emotions get people in trouble all the time. So much so they have a name for it as a defense tactic in law called a passion crime. A passion crime is an emotionally charged crash out, that often leads to violence or murder in extreme cases. In a trial of law, if it's determined the defendant was in this state at the time of the crime, the judge can lessen their penalty for the simple fact the crime wasn't premeditated. A premeditated crime is thought out by reasoning and logic and is not susceptible to this defense. Our emotions get the best of us so broadly that our own court systems are forced to acknowledge the state of our feelings in an act of "temporary insanity."

For most of us, the ability to control our emotions is extremely difficult and almost non-existent. However, for the people that have mastered the ability to control and monitor their emotions. These people are a force to be reckoned with. That's who you want to be. Someone who is in control of their emotions and will not lose control of self. People who can also monitor when they are feeling low and bring themselves back up with intention and willpower. These are the people that run the world both figuratively and literally.

Logic And Emotion Harmonized

Now, let's bring this altogether and talk about how logic and emotion help create our reality together. Like Men and Women, logic and emotion complement each other. The weakness of one is the strength of the other. As discussed, logic has very little imagination, so emotion has to account for this. Our emotions produce the thoughts and energy the Universe requires to reflect our own reality back to us. Emotions are FULL of imagination. An intentional manifestor uses emotion to report to the Universe what he or she wants, and in return must use logic to acknowledge it in the present. When we use our logic to acknowledge what we want, (especially if it isn't currently in our present), then emotion projects back out to do its work. This is the dance logic and emotion conduct in harmony. Here's the kicker, as discussed in earlier chapters, you are all doing this whether it is intentional or not. For instance, let's say you are feeling an emotion such as anger. It doesn't matter what you're angry about. Your angry thoughts and energy go out into the Universe, it reflects it back at you, you acknowledge it, and the emotion goes back out again. Rinse, wash and repeat. It's an infinite loop until the loop is broken at some point. You have chosen to remain angry and let the Universe know you currently wish to dwell in anger. This will result in manifesting scenarios in your immediate future that will piss you off. Use your logic to break the loop, acknowledge that you don't want to be angry, project the emotion and watch the magic happen. Remember, you wish to be an intentional manifestor as opposed to an unintentional manifestor. Both are manifesting their own reality, but one knows how they are doing it and why. When you learn to harness your logic and emotions to your benefit, you will see in real time how fast reality bends to your will. It does take some practice obviously. Remember, on the surface, logic and emotion seem to be mortal enemies and always working against each other but the truth is we couldn't perceive our reality without both of them. We are bound here to experience and witness duality and make choices between the supposed binary options, but when we understand the difference between choice and harmony, there is nothing that can get in our way.

Logic vs Emotion

LUCID CONCLUSIONS

Logic vs Emotion

11

The Outcome Architect

The Outcome Architect

YOU are your own Outcome Architect. Several years ago, I met with my brother in New York while I was traveling for work (I lived in Virginia at the time). We met in Manhattan and kicked it for a few hours and talked about life and things. We were very different mentally and we still are to this day for the most part. I believe we haven't had a deep conversation like this since, probably because this is when he learned I completely lost all my marbles, but I digress. I can't remember how we got on the topic, but I remember somehow Angelina Jolie came up in the conversation. In some form or fashion, we stumbled upon courting or dating her or the possibilities of such a feat. Immediately my brother went into impossibility mode. "People like us could never get someone like Angelina Jolie, how could you even think that?" It was this statement that immediately brought my mind to thinking about how I could make this happen.

"Well, for starters" I told him, "Yes, we can, and it's not as difficult as you would think. First, we know who Angelina Jolie is, and the type of person she would most likely go for. A handsome, chisel bodied actor of sorts, or at least a person high up in the movie industry such as a director or producer. We know she's in Hollywood and she's around powerful and very famous men all the time." I went on about figuring out the type of person Angelina Jolie would be attracted to and how that's the easy part. Next was comparing ourselves to this potential mate that she would consider dating. Obviously at that moment neither of us fit those criteria, but if one of us were really adamant about dating Angelina Jolie or an equivalent, we would do what we must to match the frequency of a person that fits her criteria. As the discussion progressed, I broke down what it would take to get in her line of sight. Take acting classes. Work out. Become passionate about acting and/or becoming a serious thespian. Audition for TV and movie roles. Build out an acting career and align yourself with people that work or have worked with her in the industry. Perhaps become associates with past acquaintances of hers or even current friends. And that was just choosing the actor route.

    I then went into a side bar plan about if we chose the director or movie producer route and what it would take to achieve that. I went through lengthy plans on the spot of how if I were to really want to date her what I would do to best position myself on how to do it. I really thought I was dropping game. I looked over at him and I could tell he really started to question if he knew me at all. In my mind, I was open to infinite possibilities, and I was conjuring how it could be done, and in my heart, dating Angelina Jolie didn't seem like such a farfetched feat at all. In fact, I honestly felt it was an achievable 3-5 year plan at max. Most would call this delusion, but this is the

An Elusive Perspective

mindset of an achiever and optimist that would not allow difficult obstacles or even time to get in the way of success. Granted, this is all predicated on if Angelina Jolie would even be available or interested, of course. This isn't the blueprint on how to manipulate your way into someone's heart. The good thing about this plan is even if you couldn't get Angelina Jolie herself, there are a plethora of other gorgeous actresses you could find yourself among to court instead. I say all that to say, it wasn't necessarily all about her, but about elevating my mindset into the type of person that an Angelina Jolie type would be interested in. The alternative would be the lack of even trying, throwing up my hands, giving up and saying well I could never get a woman like that based on who I am (now) so why should I even try? That energy is the exact type of energy that manifests the opposite of an "Angelina Jolie" in your life. I wouldn't know because my Wife is absolutely gorgeous.

The Outcome Architect

For most people, the idea of elevating themselves is such "An Elusive Perspective." It is absolutely foreign. They can be faced with a question intended to open their mind and never see the opportunity presented in front of them. The opportunity of conjuring thoughts and ideas which provide the foundation of manifestation in their reality. Elevation doesn't mean money, or women, or men, or material things at all. It means living the life you want on your terms. Everyone has their own version of success. I remember a story told about John Lennon when he was in school. The teacher assigned a paper in which the students were to write about what they wanted to be when they grew up. John wrote in his paper that he simply wanted to be happy. The teacher looked at his paper and told him he didn't understand the assignment, he quipped back that she didn't understand life.

This dialogue happens to a lot of us. We may know what makes us personally happy but sometimes don't understand others have different definitions of happiness. You, as your own personal outcome architect, are free to define happiness for yourself. There is a lot of pressure from the matrix to go out and hustle to make lots of money. Most of us are trained to think that money is all we need to be happy. That is a matrix default program. Money is simply a tool. It can be used as a tool for happiness, but it can also be used for nefarious purposes as we are all aware. And for those who do wish to obtain money to pursue happiness, there is nothing wrong with that either and know it is just as obtainable as your next breath.

My hope is that by bringing to your attention these illusive illusions and breaking down certain matrix programs that you can begin your awakening process and truly find what it is that makes YOU happy as opposed to what everyone else believes or what the matrix wants you to think. We've broken down lies about our media, our food, our social issues, our health, and our environments and upbringing. We exposed these limiting lies and provided guidance on how to identify and use discernment on news headlines and media stories. We talked about objective reality and subjective reality and the difference and relationship between the two. We explained how the Universe actually provides abundance for us all, but that we only have to acknowledge it and understand it's here for *US*. We learned the matrix has an agenda and it performs it well. It masks truth from us, it deceives us, and it seeks to project the worst out of us. It tells us that we are hated, and that we should be bitter and hate our fellow man. The matrix tells us that there is no such thing as abundance and there is only lack everywhere. The entire agenda of this matrix is to lie, deceive and oppress. And although we know this now, and it seems the limitations and boundaries surround and engulf us, it is our minds that can break us free. You *ARE FREE*. Your mind is unconquerable. You were born in a prison of illusion but now you see IT!

Take this new awakening and use it to your advantage and know you are a limitless light being. There is no enemy out to get you. There is no lack of resources negatively affecting your life. You have the personal relationships you want. Your health is perfect. Your finances are amazing. Your future is secure. Any dream or vision you have is yours for the taking. Know this and it shall be. Reject this and you will continue to manifest whatever it is the matrix tells you to. You will continue to believe in oppressive lies about your fellow man. You will continue to be deceived into belief systems that were constructed for your enslavement. You will inadvertently adopt limiting ideologies that cause you to hate others who seem different from you but really aren't. Reject the illusive illusions and peer through the veil. Open your mind to the endless possibilities this life has to offer and reject fear of failure. Make a commitment to practice this for a solid two years and watch in real time how much your life will change. I promise you, you won't lose anything but gain the world!

An Elusive Perspective

Books You Should Read

The Secret – Rhonda Byrnes
    https://amzn.to/41tAhGN

The World is a Mirror – Nada Amari
    https://amzn.to/41pflQV

The Biology of Belief – Bruce H. Lipton
    https://amzn.to/4goYRwl

Think and Grow Rich – Napoleon Hill
    https://amzn.to/4gnDLyF

The Source Field Investigations – David Wilcock
    https://amzn.to/4g3lCWW

The Motivation Manifesto – Brendan Burchard
    https://amzn.to/3BgwBxk

Livingood Daily – Dr. Livingood
    https://amzn.to/3ZEGkqy

To DAD – I know you're proud and watching over all of us. Thank you for instilling in us what you could with the time you had. I think about you often.

To MOM – You raised four crazy boys, and you did it with love, grace and patience! You listen to my ideas and theories and perhaps think I'm crazy at times, but you never judge and for that I am eternally grateful!
    P.S. - I tried to make sure the first few lines were catchy just for you!

To my WIFE – I wouldn't be who I am today without you. You helped me view the world in a way I could've never seen for myself and unlocked my mind several times over. Thank you.

To my SON – You are going to change the World! The Earth isn't ready for you and what you're going to bring here! Never forget this!

To my BROTHERS – I know I can get preachy and annoying, I only do it because I want better for all of us. At anytime you can tell me to just shut up lol.

About the Author

Franklin Orozco was born in the Bronx, NY to Puerto Rican parents. Like most of us, he only knew poverty and struggle for the first 20+ years of his life. In his late 20's, he began his awakening process and sought truth and relevance on Earth.

Soon after asking the Universe for help, resources and information flowed towards him. He then began to understand in depth how to take the reins and attract circumstances and opportunities that he desired.

His mission today is to share knowledge and insight that can truly help others understand how to take full advantage of their true power and escape the matrix.

Frank hosts a few podcasts in his spare time. The first is "Lucid Perspective." A weekly podcast with his Wife, Reese, where they speak about marriage and relationships.

The second podcast is "Figuring Shxt Out", with his co-host King Arthur. On "Figuring Shxt Out" Frank and Arthur speak with entrepreneurs and business owners who have valuable information to share about becoming financially free.

The last and third podcast is "Figuring Conspiracy Shxt Out", where Frank, Arthur and conspiracy expert Heru speak about trending and classic conspiracy theories.

For more info on Frank and his social media links please see below!

Lucid Perspective
        Youtube: @lucidperspective111
        Instagram: @lucidperspective
        Tiktok: @lucidperspective111
        Rumble: LucidPerspective

The Figuring Shxt Out Podcast:
        Youtube: @figureshxtout
        Instagram: @figureshxtout
        Tiktok: @figureshxtout
        Rumble: FiguringConspiracyShxtOut

Personal social media:
        Instagram: @BuneeFlacs
        Facebook: CyberBunee